## Sean Mathias

Sean Mathias is an internationally acclaimed, award-winning director of theatre and film.

He has worked extensively at the National Theatre, in the West End, and on Broadway, as well as in theatres across the United States, Australia, South Africa, the United Kingdom, Ireland, France, and New Zealand.

Sean has directed two feature films, *Bent* and, more recently, *Hamlet*. He also directed two productions for NT Live, including Harold Pinter's *No Man's Land*.

In addition to directing, Sean wrote the groundbreaking BBC film *The Lost Language of Cranes* and is the author of several plays, including his Swansea-based work *A Prayer for Wings*.

His play *Swansea Boy*, which he first workshopped 35 years ago at the National Theatre Studio, is now receiving its long-awaited debut production.

Sean lives on the Gower Coast with his partner, Paul, and their three dogs.

First published in the UK in 2025 by Aurora Metro Publications Ltd.

Based at Books on the Rise, 80 Hill Rise, Richmond, TW10 6UB UK

www.aurorametro.com   info@aurorametro.com

FB/AuroraMetroBooks  Twitter/X @aurorametro
Instagram aurora_metro

*Swansea Boy* copyright ©2025 Sean Mathias

Cover designed by Aurora Metro copyright ©2025 Aurora Metro Publications Ltd.

Production editor: Ava Holst-Roness

All rights are strictly reserved.

For rights enquiries including performing rights, please contact the author's agent: Anthony Joblin AJoblin@unitedagents.co.uk

No part of this publication may be reproduced, stored in or introduced into a retrieval system, or transmitted in any form, or by any means (electronic, mechanical, photocopying, recording or otherwise) without the prior permission of the publisher. Any person who does any unauthorised act in relation to this publication may be liable to criminal prosecution and civil claims for damages.

This paperback is sold subject to the condition that it shall not, by way of trade or otherwise, be lent, resold, hired out, or otherwise circulated without the publisher's prior consent in any form of binding or cover other than that in which it is published and without a similar condition being imposed on the subsequent purchaser.

Printed in the UK by 4edge printers on sustainably resourced paper.

ISBNs:

(print)  978-1-911501-26-8

(ebook) 978-1-911501-27-5

# SWANSEA BOY

## by

## Sean Mathias

AURORA METRO BOOKS

*For Ian Charleson*

## **CONTENTS**

About the Company 6

Biographies 9

About the Play 14

*Swansea Boy* 15

## COMPANY INFORMATION

Cainen Productions was founded in 2024 by Mark Cainen, whose passion for theatre led him to produce a world premiere of *Swansea Boy*. Collaborating with writer and director Sean Mathias, they assembled a terrific cast and dedicated creative team, to ensure that every element of *Swansea Boy* would be shared with all audiences.

*Swansea Boy* is not just a play—it is a testament to the enduring power of theatre to captivate audiences, spark conversation, and leave a lasting impact.

Cainen Productions represents a commitment to powerful storytelling, innovation, and artistic collaboration. As it moves forward, it aims to continue pushing creative boundaries, ensuring that its inaugural production serves as a foundation for future theatrical endeavours that inspire and resonate with audiences.

www.cainenproductions.com

## Volcano Theatre Company

The Volcano Theatre is an ideal venue for staging *Swansea Boy,* offering a dynamic and immersive space that enhances the production's unique storytelling approach. Known for its bold and experimental performances, Volcano Theatre provides an atmospheric setting that aligns perfectly with the themes and style of the play.

One of the key advantages of this venue is its adaptable space, which allows *Swansea Boy* to be performed in a promenade style. This means that rather than a traditional static stage setup, audiences can move through different areas of the theatre, becoming more engaged with the unfolding narrative. The versatility of the space enables the production to create an intimate and interactive experience, drawing the audience deeper into the world of the play.

Volcano Theatre's innovative approach to theatre-making, combined with its distinctive venue layout, makes it an exciting and fitting location for *Swansea Boy.* The venue's commitment to pushing creative boundaries and fostering new artistic voices further reinforces its suitability for a production that aims to be both powerful and immersive.

**www.volcanotheatre.wales**

## COMPANY INFORMATION

## CAST AND CREATIVES

**LLINOS DANIEL – MAM**
**SEBASTIAN ISAAC – COLIN**
**ALISON LENIHAN – AICHA**
**MATT OLSEN – ARI**
**STEFAN PEJIC – DAD**
**ELIZA TEALE – SHELLEY**
**CAMPBELL WALLACE – JAMES**

**WRITER & DIRECTOR – SEAN MATHIAS**
**PRODUCER – MARK CAINEN**
**SET AND COSTUME DESIGNER – LEE NEWBY**
**LIGHTING DESIGNER – JAMIE PLATT**
**SOUND DESIGNER – TONY DAVIES**

*Acknowledgements:*

We are grateful to all our supporters, sponsors, and investors who have played a vital role in bringing this production to life. Your generosity and belief in this project have made it possible for this story to be told on stage.

Many thanks to: The Ambassador Theatre Group Producer's Grant, whose funding has been instrumental in helping us develop and stage this work; Bill Kenwright Ltd for their incredibly generous investment; The Welsh Arts Council, whose financial support and guidance have been invaluable in making this production a reality; Butterfield Morgan Accountants and Swansea.com.

Thank you for being part of this journey.

## BIOGRAPHIES

## CAST

### LLINOS DANIEL – MAM

Llinos Daniel is a Welsh actress trained at Royal Holloway University of London and Webber Douglas Academy of Dramatic Art. Her television and film appearances include roles in *Hamlet* alongside Sir Ian McKellen, *Wolf, Hinterland, Torchwood,* and *Pobol y Cwm*. In theatre, Llinos has collaborated with companies such as Lighthouse Theatre, National Theatre Wales, and Theatr Na Nóg. She has worked with Sir Ian McKellen on productions of *Hamlet* and *The Cherry Orchard* at Theatre Royal, Windsor, directed by Sean Mathias. Additionally, she portrayed Mam in Mathias's play *A Prayer for Wings*. Beyond acting, Llinos has directed productions such as *The Butterfly Hunter* and *O Little Town of Aberystwyth* and is also a singer and harpist.

### SEBASTIAN ISAAC – COLIN

Sebastian Isaac is a recent graduate of The Royal Welsh College of Music & Drama, completing his acting training in 2022. During his studies, he performed in productions such as *Really Bad, Indecent, Dream, Grimm Tales, Sweat,* and *Romeo & Juliet* with the National Youth Theatre. His screen work includes appearances in *Same But Different* (AFAN ARTS) and *Cardiff I Love You* (BBC Wales). *Swansea Boy* marks Sebastian's professional theatre debut, reflecting his dedication and emerging talent in the performing arts.

## COMPANY INFORMATION

### ALISON LENIHAN – AICHA

Alison is a Welsh actress active in theatre, film, and television. She is notably recognised for her role in Channel 4's BAFTA-nominated series *The Dog House*, where she combined her passion for rehoming rescue dogs with her television work. Her theatre repertoire includes leading roles in *Yap! Yap! Yap!* with GAGGLE, and Shakespearean characters such as Lady Macbeth, Lady Capulet, and Montjoy with Fluellen Theatre Company. Alison's film credits encompass *Conjuring the Dead* (Netflix), *Tin Dancing Shoes* (BBC Wales), *The Wedding Car* (BBC Wales), *The Cleansing* (Tornado Films), and *Heart of Steel* (Copper Films). Holding a BA (Hons) in English and Film, she also facilitates drama workshops and engages in pottery as a hobby.

### MATT OLSEN – ARI

Matt is a Welsh actor who graduated from Italia Conti. During his studies, he performed in productions such as *Almost, Maine* at the Edinburgh Fringe festival, *The Pride* and *The Winter's Tale*. Television credits include *Ghosts* (BBC) and *Miss Scarlet and the Duke* (Alibi). Matt is thrilled to be a part of *Swansea Boy,* marking his Welsh theatre debut in the city he was born where he first fell in love with acting.

### STEFAN PEJIC – DAD

Stefan, born in Swansea, is a versatile entertainer with a career spanning stage and screen. His television credits

include roles in *Casualty, Sherlock, Doctors"* (BBC), *Nuts & Bolts* (ITV), and *The Rezort* (Netflix/Amazon). In theatre, he has portrayed characters such as Mercutio in *Romeo & Juliet* and Professor Moriarty in *Sherlock Holmes*. Stefan also runs Pejic Productions, delivering immersive corporate entertainment worldwide, and is set to star as Tommy Cooper in *COOPER! THE MUSICAL*.

## ELIZA TEALE – SHELLEY

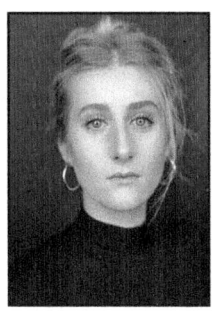

Eliza is a recent graduate of the Royal Welsh College of Music and Drama. She recently appeared in Sean Mathias' production of *Filumena* at the Theatre Royal Windsor. Her theatre credits include Elizabeth in *The Welkin* and Grace in *Mad Margot* both at The Sherman Theatre, Cardiff. Eliza holds a Bachelor's degree in Drama with French from the University of Manchester, where she was involved in performing, producing, and directing new writing shows.

## CAMPBELL WALLACE – JAMES

Campbell is a graduate of the Royal Welsh College of Music and Drama. His theatre credits include the role of Romeo in *First Encounters: Romeo and Juliet*, as well as performances in *Mudflats* by Chris McCabe, *Lord of the Flies*, and *The Book of Dust: La Belle Sauvage*. Known for his authentic and captivating performances, Campbell is excited to be part of *Swansea Boy*.

## CREATIVES
### MARK CAINEN – PRODUCER

Mark is a writer and producer who is passionate about bringing original stories to the stage and screen. His most recent play, *Conviction*, received critical acclaim when it was staged in 2024 at Swansea's Grand Theatre. It is due to tour in 2026.

In addition to his work as a playwright and producer, Mark teaches scriptwriting at Cardiff Metropolitan University and the University of the West of England (UWE), helping to develop the next generation of writers.

Having recently completed his Ph.D. at Swansea University, Mark is particularly interested in bridging the gap between academia and the practical realities of getting work published and produced. He is committed to helping writers navigate the industry, bringing theoretical knowledge into real-world application.

Mark lives in Swansea with his wife, Claire, and their two children.

### SET AND COSTUME DESIGNER – LEE NEWBY

Lee is a set and costume designer who graduated from the Liverpool Institute for Performing Arts (LIPA) in 2011, where he developed a strong foundation in theatre design. His career has since taken him across the globe, contributing to a wide range of productions including plays, musicals, dance, and circus performances.

He has had the opportunity to work with director Sean Mathias on several projects, beginning with *Gently Down the Stream* (Park Theatre, 2017). Their collaboration continued with *A Prayer for Wings* at Volcano Theatre in Swansea (2019), a co-production with Volcano and Swansea Grand Theatre marking the city's 50th anniversary. Newby also designed the sets for Mathias' inaugural summer season at Theatre Royal Windsor in 2021, including *Hamlet* and *The Cherry Orchard,* both featuring a repertory company led by Sir Ian McKellen.

Notable theatre credits include his West End debut with James Graham's Olivier Award-winning comedy *Labour of Love* (Noël Coward Theatre, 2017); *The Life I Lead* (Wyndham's Theatre, 2019), *The Last Five Years* (Garrick Theatre, 2022), *The Enfield Haunting* (Ambassadors Theatre, 2024), and the upcoming *The Last Laugh* (Noël Coward Theatre, 2025).

## JAMIE PLATT – LIGHTING DESIGNER

Jamie is a theatre lighting designer based in London and has designed lighting for plays, musicals, operas, and dance at venues across the UK and around the world. He trained at the Royal Welsh College of Music & Drama, is a professional member of the Association for Lighting Production and Design and has twice been elected to sit on the Equity Directors & Designers committee.

He has been nominated for five Off-West End Awards, a Knight of Illumination Award, and a Broadway World Award, and in 2013 won the ALD's ETC Award and RWCMD's Carne Award.

Notable productions include: *The Last Five Years* (West End & International Tour); *Jellyfish* (National Theatre); *Midnight in the Garden of Good and Evil* (Goodman Theatre, Chicago); *RIDE* (Old Globe, San Diego) and *Something Rotten! & Pippin* (Theatre Royal Drury Lane).

## SOUND DESIGNER – TONY DAVIES

Tony has spent his working life in theatre. This has included touring the UK, working in London's West End and three decades as head of sound at Swansea Grand Theatre. This included over thirty Rep seasons and pantomimes. A year at Disney Cruise Line as head of sound followed before continuing his career as a freelance sound designer.

## ABOUT SWANSEA BOY

I began writing *Swansea Boy* as a response to the AIDS pandemic and as a way to explore another play in the Swansea idiom following the success of *A Prayer for Wings*.

The story follows Colin, a budding artist who spends his days idling on a Gower beach, dreaming of a more bohemian life in London. However, his Welsh family pressures him to finish school and pursue a more conventional path. His friend Shelley amuses him, but she cannot fulfill his growing sense of longing. A sexual encounter with James, another boy his age, gives Colin the courage to leave behind the beauty of the Gower Coast and head to London.

In the city, Colin discovers a world more elusive and unsettling than he had imagined. As the AIDS crisis unfolds, he navigates life with fear and trepidation, yet remains true to himself by choosing a path of sexual safety and finding the courage to come out to his family.

Later, in a small Moroccan seaside town, Colin lives with James, who is slowly succumbing to HIV. Amidst the exotic beauty of his new home, filled with rare creatures and constant sunlight, Colin creates his own bohemian haven. Displaying a maturity beyond his years, he faces the harsh realities of mortality with compassion and resilience.

– **Sean Mathias**
(Writer and Director)

# SWANSEA BOY

## Sean Mathias

The play received its premiere production at Volcano Theatre, Swansea on March 7th, 2025.

Characters:

**COLIN**  A Swansea boy.
**SHELLEY** A Swansea girl.
**MAM**  Colin's mother.
**DAD**  Colin's father.
**ARI**  A Greek boy.
**JAMES**  Another Swansea boy.
**AICHA**  A Moroccan woman.

*Author's note:* Punctuation marks are placed according to the speech patterns of the characters. For instance, commas are often missed out. This is intentional.

# ACT ONE

*A boy sitting in the sand dunes in South Wales. The sound of gulls dies away.*

**COLIN**   My cock spurted its fountain. Blood red it was. Blood red the colour of blood. Bloody blood. Bloody blood red blood, bleeding all over my hand and trickling down the sides of my stiff and worried bloody cock. I don't know where it came from. Except inside me. I was just giving myself a hand-job at the time. There wasn't any pain. And there wasn't any pleasure. I wanted to bottle it and paint a canvas. Daub it all over a white canvas. Smear the bloody blood red bleeding blood all over the speckled fleckled whitey white sheet of newness, of nothing. When I realised I hadn't fainted, I looked down at my cock, to examine. But there was nothing. Nothing to behold. My cock was still attached to my balls, still attached to my groin, still attached to me. And I was attached to it. Very attached actually. No cuts. No wounds. No permanent damage. Something inside me. Tried to get out. Something inside me not right. That's how I remember it.

*Enter SHELLEY.*

**SHELLEY** Colin! Colin!

**COLIN**   That's Shelley. Common as muck but heart of steel.

**SHELLEY** Where are you? Come on! Come in the water.

Come in the sea. Come on Colin. Colin. Where are you? There you are, Colin. What the hell are you doing over by there then? Ooh Colin there's blood all over your hand. You cut you'self babes. Colin look at you.

**COLIN**   It's nothing. I cut myself on a bit of glass.

**SHELLEY** Come in the water. Wash you'self clean. We can play with each other. I'll let you touch me down there.

**COLIN**   In the sea?

**SHELLEY** It's best in the water.

**COLIN**   Why's that?

**SHELLEY** The motion ... motion of the ocean. That's it. It swills around you. Makes you feel horny.

**COLIN**   You're a randy little sod.

**SHELLEY**   So are you. You're a randy little sod. With a big cock. Come on Col. Let's go in the sea.

**COLIN**   I couldn't get an hard-on in there.

**SHELLEY** Why not?

**COLIN**   It's too bleeding cold. That sea.

**SHELLEY** I'll suck your cock under water.

**COLIN**   You'll asphyxiate. Don't be filthy, Shell.

**SHELLEY** Common as muck aren't I? Everyone says so.

**COLIN**   How many boys' cocks have you sucked?

**SHELLEY** Hardly any.

**COLIN**   Get on.

**SHELLEY** What's it to you anyhow?

**COLIN**   You wanna be careful.

**SHELLEY** Why's that?

**COLIN** Diseases.

**SHELLEY** Get on. I haven't sucked that many.

**COLIN** It only takes one Shell.

**SHELLEY** I've only sucked three and one of them was yours.

**COLIN** Well you want to watch it. You're only sixteen.

**SHELLEY** Come on Col. Let's go in the sea. I'm bored ...

**COLIN** You're just randy.

**SHELLEY** So what?

**COLIN** What's my mam and dad doing?

**SHELLEY** Eating. Keith's playing football.

**COLIN** With his mates?

**SHELLEY** How come you haven't got any mates Col?

**COLIN** Dunno.

**SHELLEY** What'll you do when you leaves school?

**COLIN** Dunno. I'd like to be a painter.

**SHELLEY** Painter and decorator!

**COLIN** No! Proper painter. An artist.

**SHELLEY** What d'you mean?

**COLIN** Shelley don't be stupid. A painter. Gaugin. Picasso. Andy Warhol.

**SHELLEY** Andy Warhol I've heard of him. *(Sings)*
"Andy Warhol looks a scream
Hang him on my wall
Andy Warhol silver screen
Can't tell him apart at all."

Come on Col. Let's go in the sea. The sun will start dipping soon.

**COLIN**   And you want a bit o' cock.

**SHELLEY** Don't be disgusting Colin. (*A pause.*) How many girls have you...?

**COLIN**   You're the second.

**SHELLEY** Blimey you're a shy one.

**COLIN**   Maybe.

**SHELLEY** Come on. I'll race you down the water. Give you a submarine blow-job.

**COLIN**   You're a filthy girl.

**SHELLEY** Common as muck me. That's what the boys love. Come on Col.

*They are gone. The sound of laughter and kids playing is heard. This is replaced with the sound of waves crashing, then gulls screeching and finally the magic sound of a flute whistles over everything. Throughout these sounds the light dims from orange sunlight to a duskiness and then to dark navy night. The sounds die away. The sun rises on a new day. COLIN wanders into the sand dunes.*

**COLIN**   It's been raining all week. Bleeding well pissing down. It always pisses down in the school holidays. My cock's alright. Haven't had no problems with it since. Mind you I haven't had a wank. Been too frightened to touch it. Sounds stupid, I know but I was afraid it was going to fall off. Thought God was punishing me. Anyhow I haven't touched it for a week but there's been no more blood. When I was thirteen I was playing in the yard one day. At school. It was in February. I hate February. It's suicide month is

February. It had been snowing for about ten days. We'd had a couple days off school – snow was so bad. But we were back now. Worst luck. And the snow was going all slushy. It was grey and messy. And someone threw a snowball in my face. Playing they was mind. It hit me right in the face. A bloody bleeding white, frosty white snowball. Right under the left eye. And some blood trickled down my cheek and dropped onto the snowy ground. Blood red blood on snow white snow. Red on white. This bloody huge thing grew on my face. On my cheek. Big red lump. No bloody bugger knew what it was. No bloody doctors, Mam nor Dad. I hate school. Can't wait to leave. The only thing I enjoy is art. It's a place I can day-dream and make my day-dreams into something. The mark healed eventually. But I'll never forget that snowball.

*Enter MAM.*

**MAM** Colin! Colin! Where are you! Colin! It's nearly lunch-time love. Oh there you are lovey. What you doing over by there?

**COLIN** Day-dreaming.

**MAM** Oh I'm all out of breath love. Them dunes are uphill struggle. They really stretch them leg muscles to oblivion. Ooh let me catch my breath Col. What you doing by here love? All on your only. All on your tod. Shift over love. I'll sit down.

**COLIN** There's plenty of room Mam.

**MAM** Our Keith's playing football. He never stops kicking that ball. Racing round that sand. Your father's sleeping. Snoring on the beach. Puts me to shame. Oh it's embarrassing love. Snoring like a fog-horn on the beach. These three kiddies came by and they was pointing and giggling. Pointing at your dad lying there snoring on the beach. And his stomach's out here. Puts me to shame. I said, "Clear off you little monkeys." Cheeky beggars they are. Then he lets out this huge snore. Sounded like a bloody liner. And then you'll never guess. He farts. Lying there like a beached whale snoring, and he farts. "Oh, I'm off," I says. I'm not having him put me to shame. I don't come down the Gower Coast for him to lie there farting in his slumbers.

**COLIN**  We all fart when we're asleep Mam.

**MAM**  Don't talk daft. I never do. I thought, "I'll go for a little walk. Find our Col." And you're over by here. On your tod in the dunes. I ask you.

**COLIN**  I like it.

**MAM**  I loves the Gower. Makes a change from Boots. I'd like to give up that job Colin. Selling Tampax to bloody cows all day long. It's not my idea of an holiday.

**COLIN**  Well work isn't meant to be an holiday Mam.

**MAM**  Your father makes good money. I don't have to work. Gets me out the house that's all. Now that Keith's fourteen he can be tidy on his own. Maybe they could shift me to C.D.'s. I could fancy that. I'd play Frank Sinatra all day long. I loves the Gower. It's a wonder we never went in for a caravan. (*A pause.*) What are you doing up here Colin? On your own. Why don't you play football with our Keith?

**COLIN**  I can't play football. I'm no good at it.

**MAM**  Nonsense. Any beggar can kick a ball. I reckon my legs are going varicose Col. It's hideous sight. Varicose veins. Well what d'you expect standing on your feet all day long in Boots? Husband who only eats snores and farts. Dad's well over weight. And he don't do no exercise. Comes down here, don't go in the sea. At least I has a paddle. You're a good swimmer Col.

**COLIN** Alright.

**MAM** Get on. You're excellent. I watched you and Shelley. Last week. You're an excellent swimmer. And diver. You and Shelley diving underneath each other's legs. Excellent. She can stay under water for a hell of a time that girl. Where is Shell today Col?

**COLIN** She had to stop home and look after her mam.

**MAM** Poor little mite. Having a cripple mother and she the only one. She never met her dad then?

**COLIN** No, he left when the mam was pregnant.

**MAM** Poor Shelley. She's a lovely girl. But what a burden. It's not serious with you kids is it?

**COLIN** What?

**MAM** You and Shelley? You're not serious or nothing?

**COLIN** No Mam.

**MAM** Good. A cripple for a mother in-law. It's a lot to take on.

**COLIN** I'm not getting married.

**MAM** Good. I mean Shelley's a nice enough girl. But she's a bit common.

**COLIN** Ever.

**MAM** What?

**COLIN** I'm not getting married ever. I'm not Mam.

**MAM** Well you're young. There's a plenty of time yet.

**COLIN** I want to leave school. Go to art school.

**MAM** No Colin. Finish your A's love.

**COLIN** I hate it Mam. I hate school. I don't have no mates. I hate Swansea. I hate it.

**MAM** Not that old tune. God help. Here I tell you what love. Why don't you and me go away? I've saved some money. In Boots. Lets go away this summer. I fancies Greece. They say Koz is tidy. I'll treat you. You and me both. Our little treat. We'll have ten days. What you'd say?

**COLIN** Dunno.

**MAM** Your father can cater for himself. Ten days of micro won't kill him. And Keith's old enough to keep himself tidy. What d'you say Col?

**COLIN** Dunno.

**MAM** I don't know. Sometimes you're a miserable sod. Come on, my stomach's barking. Oh, I loves the Gower but I could fancy Kos. And I could use the break. Do me good to get away from your father. Course it's my treat, but there's one condition.

**COLIN** I knew it.

**MAM** Stay and finish you're A's love. Don't go racing and rushing. Come on. I made avocado and prawn sarnies. Bloody hell, these dunes are bound to be lethal for my varicose.

*They leave. The same sounds fill the air and the light changes from day to night. The light comes up on a new day and COLIN is in the dunes.*

**COLIN** Course the trouble with Shelley's blow-jobs is her teeth. She's too teethy. And too toothy too. Too many teeth. Tons and tons of shining white, whitey white toothy teeth. It's like facing a pack of piranhas. What I need see is something with a bit of expertise. Bit of a master stroke. Someone who know what's what. 'Cos I don't know what's what, that's for sure. Mam and Dad have been rowing all week. She keeps accusing him of having a fancy woman. It's daft it is. He works too hard for a bit on the side, but Mam will get into a state. I said "Mam take the poodle down the park and give over. Walk it off." But she just goes on and on. She's not yet forty and she feels it all slipping.

*DAD enters.*

**DAD**  Colin! Colin! Where are you? What the frigging hell you doing in the bastard dunes? You're always up the dunes. What the hell for Col?

**COLIN**  Dunno. I likes it.

**DAD**  Ah shift over. I'll join you.

**COLIN**  There's plenty of room Dad.

**DAD**  To tell you the truth I come up here for a bit of peace. Your mother's driving me round the bastard bend. She won't give over. Keeps going on about fantasy blondes. Wish I frigging had one. Shelley's got the hump with you. She's playing football with our Keith. She's hell of a dribbler. And she's kicking that bastard ball like she hated it. I shouted out "Here Shelley, looks like you're kicking our Colin's head the relish you're putting into that game." Gave her a good laugh. But I distracted her and she took a tackle. So I thought I'd better clear out before she gets the hump with me. I'm glad I'm not that bastard ball. Your mother won't stop eating sandwiches. Sandwiches and crisps. She just keeps stuffing her face. What the hell you plotting up here mush?

**COLIN** Dunno.

**DAD** Thinking about women is it?

**COLIN** Not exactly.

**DAD** Go on. No need to be shy with me. I don't know about this Greece trip. Mam's set her heart on it. All but booked up. Seems queer to me. You and Mam going off. Leaving me and Keith on our bastard tod. I'm no Egon frigging Ronay. Keith'll be subsisting on chips and cornflakes. He'll be a pimply little sod by the end of ten days. Why don't we all go if we're going?

**COLIN** Dunno Dad.

**DAD** Yeah. Well I can't take time off work anyhow. Though it's a wonder she won't take both you boys. There's no swaying her.

**COLIN** Dunno that I even want to go.

**DAD** Well no bugger's forcing you. Stop by here if you don't fancy going.

**COLIN** No I do.

**DAD** But?

**COLIN** Well.

**DAD** But?

**COLIN** It's just that she's blackmailing me that's all.

**DAD** If you goes it's A levels? No A's no Greece?

**COLIN** That's it.

**DAD** Well fair enough innit? Mam's got her methods I know, but let's be fair, it's fair enough innit? I mean if you don't do your A's, what frigging use it going to be? Life. Life without further education? Look at me. I sell cars. Oh granted I got my own business.

I done well. We got a nice life. Two videos. Two cars; well that's the least I could manage eh? Mam gets a new dishwasher every eighteen months. I've put a deposit down on that jacuzzi for the bathroom. Mam fancies it like hell. Says it'll soothe her muscles. "The Whirlpool". We got all the cons. But let's be fair all I do is sell bloody cars. Four C.S.E.'s and I'm a used car salesman.

**COLIN** You sell new cars an' all.

**DAD** I'm a disappointed man, Col. Two or three A's and you'll be tidy. You'll be on the road. No A's whatsoever and you'll get as far as the M.4, test-driving for me.

**COLIN** That's not the only two "routes."

**DAD** But with a few qualifications things'll open up.

**COLIN** What things? There's blokes out there with big degrees. They're over-qualified. Can't get arrested.

**DAD** There's always an exception, I'll grant you that. But in principle Col. Finish your schooling son and go on a bit further.

**COLIN** But I fancies art school Dad.

**DAD** Don't talk bastard soft. Where's that gonna get you?

**COLIN** I don't know Dad, we'll see.

**DAD** Aye. Well am I paying for this Greece trip or not?

**COLIN** Mam says it's her treat.

**DAD** What the hell is she gonna scoff up from?

**COLIN** She reckons she's got a nest egg.

**DAD** She's a sly one her. More like *she* got a bit on the side. Eh son?

**COLIN** Maybe.

**DAD** Ha! What about you and Shell then? Going strong is it? Strong and steady?

**COLIN** Christ! Everyone's on about me and Shelley. Shelley's just a mate. Alright?

**DAD** Calm down. No problems. No need for you to be going steady yet. You're young son.

**COLIN** Well I'm not going steady with no girls. So everyone can just leave off.

**DAD** Keep your hair on. Don't fly off the bastard handle.

**COLIN** I'm going down the water.

**DAD** Aye alright. So what's the bargain then? We got a deal?

**COLIN** Taramasalata and A level French. It's an odd mixture.

**DAD** Take the trip son. Do you the power.

**COLIN** We'll see.

*He goes. The light fades then rises again on a brilliant Greek sunny day. At the same time the sound of laughter on a Greek beach fills the air mingling with Greek music.*

*COLIN enters with a gaudy umbrella and painting equipment. He fixes the umbrella into the sand.*

**COLIN** I'm plastered in number sixteen. Blinking soft idea. Coming here in August. It's bleeding four o'clock in the afternoon and it's ninety-six degrees. That's supposed to be mild, for the season. Mam looked like a lobster by day three. She's toned down a bit now. She's having whale of a time. We met this bloke, Aristopolous. I think that's his name. We can't get our Swansea tongues wrapped round their Greek words. And there's a limit to his English. He and Mam have gone swimming. I reckon she fancies him. She never stops flirting. And I think he fancies her too. Anyhow there's no harm in any of it. Gives me a chance to do some painting. (*He sets up a small easel and starts to paint.*) The colours are absolutely brilliant over here. All blues and greens. And the light. It's beyond all credence. Shining down. Shining slyly on my bluey brush. We get up about eightish 'cos it's so hot. We have a swim. My crawl's getting quite tidy. Course the sea's superb. Really hot. And it's gorgeous colour. Millions of colours. Swimming together. If you go out a bit you can see all the fishes. Down by the rocky bits. Millions of fishes covered in billions of stripes. Billions of beautiful colours swimming together and against one another. We hire the snorkels and stay in the water for hours. But you got to watch your shoulders. The sun's really burning. Piping hot orange it is. I tell you what, I feels horny over here. Here in Kos. It's the warmth I reckon. Keep getting hard-ons. Can get an hard-on in the sea over here. Mam keeps talking to all these girls for me. It's so bleeding embarrassing. Keeps on shaming me she do. "That's a nice one for you Col." All the while she's after Aristopolous. Spiralled into a new fantasy she have. Reckons we can go about like a foursome. Mother and son all liberated like. We eat fish for tea and lots of salad. And their chips are glorious. Cooked in olive oil. They're a bit greasy but not like from the chippy. They taste healthy greasy. Greek greasy. Lots of snoozing, then back down the beach late afternoon. Every night we go to the caffs and Mam invariably gets pissed. Retsina. Bleeding poisonous it is.

*MAM and ARI enter.*

**MAM** Christ Col. I got a lingering hangover today love. Too much of that red-stinker. Ari's been teaching me backstroke. Had me flat on my back in that bay. Didn't you Ari?

**ARI** Yes.

**MAM** Blinking saucebox. I reckon we should stow him in our luggage Col. Get him down the Gower. Give your old man something to think about. Eh Ari?

**ARI** Yes. I dry you.

**MAM** Ta love. *(ARI rubs MAM with a towel.)* What you painting Col?

**COLIN** What you see really. What the eye can see.

**MAM** It's good love. You're getting good. You get a couple of decent A's and maybe I'll persuade your dad. About the art school bit.

**COLIN** I dunno Mam. I'm going to fail French. I'm useless. Useless at it.

**MAM** Don't talk soft. You work hard and you'll get the pass. Steady on Ari. Not down there love. All ticklish.

**ARI** Tick?

**MAM** Ticklish. You know love. Like this.

*She tickles ARI under the arms. He giggles.*

**ARI** Ticklish.

**MAM** That's it. A level English here we come.

**ARI** English?

**MAM** Yeah.

**ARI** English good.

**MAM** Well not bad. He'd qualify for nursery, eh Colin?

**COLIN** Mmm?

**MAM** I was saying Ari's not quite ready for A levels yet.

**COLIN** Stop going on about sodding A levels.

**MAM** Sorry I spoke. Just my little joke.

**COLIN** Well we're on a holiday alright? I don't want to keep hearing about A levels.

**MAM** Pardonnez-moi for breathing. He's a grumpy bugger, eh Ari?

**ARI** Yes.

**COLIN** I'm sorry, It's just that, well I don't know, I'm not looking forward to going back. Our last day tomorrow, it's just that, well I'd nearly forgotten about all that. Over there. Life - School. I don't want to stay on in bloody bleeding school. Bloody bleeding sodding bleeding bloody bloody bloody bloody bleeding bloody school.

*A pause.*

**MAM** You needn't tell me love. I'm dreading it. I'm going to quit Boots. I can't bear the thought of it. And having to cook again. Looking after everyone. I tell you I feels quite lazy, quite spoiled over here in Kos. I hope our Keith's walking the poodle. I've half a mind not to go back at all. To stay put by here. Let them go on with it. If it weren't for you and Keith, I tell you, I could go in for it. Running a little taverna on the island of Kos.

**COLIN**  You don't mean it.

**MAM**  Well of course I'm not going to do it. But I could fancy it I tell you. Ari?

**ARI**  Yes?

**MAM**  Let's have another swim.

**ARI**  Swim?

**MAM**  In the water. Come on. Let's go back down the bay. Come on Col. Let's go in the water.

**COLIN**  No thanks Mam. I want to stay and finish this painting. It's my last chance. You go.

**MAM**  Alright then. Come on Ari.

**ARI**  No. Tired. Sleep in sun.

**MAM**  Never. You're never tired. There's a hopeless lot. Well I fancies another swim.

*She goes. COLIN paints. ARI is lying flat on his back. After a few moments he half sits, on his elbows and watches COLIN. A long pause.*

**ARI**  You – painter?

**COLIN**  What?

**ARI**  Painter?

**COLIN**  Yes. I'm a painter. Trying to be one. I mean I'd like to be one. I'd like to go to art school. Become an artist. Therein lies a tale. Family conflict.

**ARI**  Painter?

**COLIN**  Yes, I am a painter.

**ARI**   Good painter.

**COLIN**   Well I dunno. I'm not sure really. I think I'm good. That is I'm alright. I'm probably the best in my class. But that's not saying much. The rest of them is useless. Then again I'm useless at everything else. I'm not sure really. I think I'm alright. I reckon if I work hard I'll get A level art. Maybe a good grade even. But do I want to stay on? Do I? What do you reckon Ari?

**ARI**   Good. Good painter. Very good painter.

**COLIN**   Thank you.

*A pause. COLIN paints.*

**ARI**   You – boy. *(A pause.)* Good boy.

**COLIN**   I'm sorry?

**ARI**   Yes. Very good boy.

**COLIN**   Thankyou. Not sure what I've done to deserve that. Thankyou.

**ARI**   Yes. Thankyou. Very good boy. *(A pause.)* Very good boy I like. *(He sits up.)*

**COLIN**   Thankyou. Well you're my friend too. You've been a good friend. To me and Mam. Especially Mam. Well, indirectly especially me. 'Cos to tell you the truth Ari, you've done me a big favour. Taking Mam off my hands like that. I mean it's a big relief. It's given me time to myself. To think. And paint. All in all, you've been a really good friend to us both. You must come to Swansea. We'll return the hospitality.

**ARI**   Yes. Very good boy I like.

**COLIN**   Thankyou. It's a problem this language thing. I've never had it before. But I s'pose it happens the world over. I'm always having the communication thing. The communication problem. But this is somehow different. This is not plain misunderstanding. We are completely unable to express ourselves. In words anyhow. And that's what we're used to innit? Words. Thankyou.

**ARI** You. You boy. You boy I like. *(He kneels up. COLIN stops painting.)*

**COLIN** Ari I think you're trying to tell me something and I'm really not sure what. I'm not sure what at all, but you're making me nervous.

**ARI** *(puts his hand on his crotch.)* Good. Is good here. Good for boy. You boy I like.

**COLIN** Oh Christ.

**ARI** Cock. Cock I have. Big Cock. Is good. Big Cock for boy. Boy Colin.

**COLIN** Oh my Christ. Mam. Mam where are you? I thought that was your department. I thought you were helping Ari out down there. Oh Mam I'm sorry. I've thought badly of you. I'm sorry Mam but I wish you'd come and rescue me now.

**ARI** Colin like. Is good for Colin. Ari like Colin.

**COLIN** Oh Christ I'm out of my depth. His cock is bulging. He wants an hand-job. Oh Christ Ari I thought you liked the girls? Eh? Girls Ari?

**ARI** *(grins.)* Girls. Girls is good. Boys. Boys is good. Cock is big.

**COLIN** Oh God Colin get a grip. I'm getting an hard-on. I don't know what to do. I've thought about boys' cocks. I've had hard-ons before now thinking about them, but I didn't know. Cock go down. Control yourself.

**ARI** Colin cock. Good. Is big. Ari cock big. Is good.

*ARI walks on his knees to touch COLIN. COLIN pulls away.*

**COLIN** Christ Ari. No. Not here. Oh sweet Jesus. What the frigging bleeding hell am I meant to do now? What the bleeding bloody hell do I do?

**ARI** Here. Yes. Is good. You. You touch. Nice boy. Touch Ari cock.

**COLIN** Look I'm sorry. You're very nice and very lovely. Yes lovely. You're a lovely looking man. You've got a lovely face. A lovely body. A beautiful body. Yes that's it. It's beautiful. Strong. And golden. Golden-bronzed. You're a nice man. A good friend. And a cock. Yes you've got a cock.

**ARI** Good.

**COLIN** Yes it looks good, and big. Huge almost. Hard and throbbing and oh my God. My sweet God. But I'm just not. I'm just not used. Not used to this. I'm a mixed-up, muddled-up seventeen year old who's never done this, who can't get his fantasy life in order, let alone reality, who can't allow a girl to give him a blow job let alone touch a Greek man's cock. Here. Here on the beach in Kos. I'm just not. Just not ready.

**ARI** Colin. Good boy. Good friend. No problem.

**COLIN** Oh my God I think he understands me.

**ARI** No problem. I like you.

**COLIN** Thankyou. Thankyou very much. I like you too.

**ARI** Good. Is good. Colin is good boy. Friend. Friend to Ari.

**COLIN** Yes. Good friend. Very much a good friend. Ari's friend. *(He shakes ARI's hand.)*

**ARI**   Good friend. Mi amigo. Amigo. Si.

*They smile, then laugh, shake hands vigorously and repeat the word "friend".*

*MAM enters.*

**MAM**   What the hell are you two doing? Playing silly buggers? *(They break. COLIN packs up his art work.)* Ooh I had a luscious swim. Colin I found a gorgeous girl. A gorgeous girl for you. I've made a date. She's Italian. Beautiful kid. She's meeting us at the taverna. You'll love her. Come on I'm starving. I fancies some olives and red stinker. Come on Ari. *(ARI picks up the umbrella. Colin has gathered his things.)* Her name's Daniella. Beautiful brown eyes. She's a gorgeous creature. Come on boys. Let's be having you. *(She links arms with the two men.)*

**ARI**   My Welsh family.

**MAM**   My little Greek saucebox.

*COLIN is silent. They leave. The magic flute is heard and the Greek light fades away. The light comes up on the Gower coast. The sound of the flute is replaced by gulls. It is a cloudy day. COLIN enters in long shorts and a sweat shirt. He carries a sketch book.*

**COLIN**   What a fiasco. Our last night. Mam wouldn't let up. Kept on at me to dance with Daniella. We all went down the disco and Mam was well pissed. Pie-eyed. I couldn't look at Ari after what happened. I just couldn't face him. And the stupid thing is now I can't stop thinking about him. I lie in bed at night and think about him. And think about his bulging cock. And it gives me an hard-on. In Kos I'd have sooner died than touch him but now I can't get him out of my mind. His lovely smiling Greek face.

All I dream about is getting on a plane, flying back to Kos, finding Ari and touching his cock. "Me – good boy." And wrapping myself in his arms. Lying in the dunes wrapped in his Greek warmth. It was pissing down when we landed at Gatwick. Pissing grey. After all that turquoise everything was grey. And our plane was delayed. So we didn't get to even greyer Swansea till the small grey hours.

Everyone asleep. Buddy, our grey poodle woke up and barked. That woke Dad up. He came downstairs. When he saw Mam looking all brown and healthy he looked quite randy. I don't s'pose she did nothing with Ari. I dunno, just a flirt and a cuddle. Anyhow they getting on much better now. Mam and Dad. So Mam had the right instinct. Getting away. My tan's faded. And I don't feel like painting. Just a lot of sketching. Charcoals. Keith's been selected for the Swansea Juniors. Under Fifteens. He's training now. Training all the time. He don't come down the bays no more. Shelley's decided she's not going back to school. She got her results. She got two O levels and four C.S.E.'s. Poor Shelley it's not her fault. The odds are stacked against her. Mam got her a job. Got her into Boots. She starts Monday. So the summer's over. Everything's ending. It's still August mind but the weather's like Autumn. I don't know. Ten days left and it's back to prison. Nose to the grindstone. Swatting and hating every minute of it. I want to paint!

*SHELLEY enters.*

**SHELLEY** Colin! Colin! Where are you? Over by there. Same as usual. What you doing over by there Col?

**COLIN**  I'm drawing.

**SHELLEY** Gi's a butcher's. It's great. You getting

really good Col. Ooh it's horrible day. I'm bleeding-well-nobbled.

**COLIN** Daft innit? Coming down the bays on a day like this.

**SHELLEY** Well I'm happy to in one way 'cos it's probably my last chance. I starts Monday.

**COLIN** Are you nervous?

**SHELLEY** Bleeding shitting myself. I'm cowing terrified.

**COLIN** Why Shell?

**SHELLEY** Well I've never done nothing 'cept go to school. And look after Mam. And I'm not very bright.

**COLIN** That's not true.

**SHELLEY** But I talks all common. I'm sure they gonna sack me.

**COLIN** Don't be daft. Just keep your head. Don't get in a panic. Do your best.

**SHELLEY** You're a good friend you are Col. I missed you when you was in Kos. Was you naughty? When you was there?

**COLIN** What d'you mean?

**SHELLEY** Come on. Was you wicked?

**COLIN** D'you mean sex?

**SHELLEY** Course. Feel up any girls?

**COLIN** No.

**SHELLEY** Liar.

**COLIN** I never. *(A pause.)* But I was horny.

**SHELLEY** Randy little sod. I bet you did something.

**COLIN** I didn't actually.

**SHELLEY** There's boring. Nothing happened here neither.

*COLIN stops drawing. Another pause.*

**COLIN** Actually, something did happen Shell.

**SHELLEY** I knew it. I knew it.

**COLIN** But I never did nothing.

**SHELLEY** Yeah!

**COLIN** There was this bloke.

**SHELLEY** Yeah?

**COLIN** Became a friend of me and Mam.

**SHELLEY** Yeah?

**COLIN** His name was Aristopolous. I reckon he fancied me.

**SHELLEY** Never?

**COLIN** And what's more I reckon Mam fancied him.

**SHELLEY** Never!

**COLIN** Anyhow it was all quite harmless.

**SHELLEY** Yeah.

**COLIN** And on the day before we left.

**SHELLEY** Yeah?

**COLIN** Mam was swimming.

**SHELLEY** Yeah?

**COLIN** And Ari was lying on the beach. And I was painting.

**SHELLEY** Yeah?

**COLIN** And suddenly, he got this big hard-on. *(SHELLEY smiles vacantly.)* And he wanted me to play with his cock.

**SHELLEY** Yeah?

**COLIN** Well that was it. I didn't.

**SHELLEY** You are joking.

**COLIN** I'm not.

**SHELLEY** A queer? He was a queer?

**COLIN** Well he was...

**SHELLEY** Eugh! There's disgusting.

**COLIN** I didn't of course. But you know what?

**SHELLEY** What?

**COLIN** I wanted to. Really. Deep down. I wanted to. And if he asked me again. All over again. I would.

*A pause. SHELLEY screams.*

**SHELLEY** Colin! Colin! There's horrible. That's cowing smegging that is. You never a queer? You never are? Oh Colin I'm shamed. You cowing can't be. I sucked your cock. You can't be? You never are. You never a queer?

**COLIN** Shelley keep your voice down. I don't know. I don't know what's what.

**SHELLEY** That's vile. That's really vile. Literally vile. That's cowing hanging that is. Minging!

**COLIN** Calm down Shelley. I don't know what I am. And I don't see what difference it makes.

**SHELLEY** But you can't be. You just can't.

**COLIN** Well what difference? What difference would

it make?

**SHELLEY** Well... well... it's the end of us for one thing. I don't know. I don't understand. Oh Colin you can't be?

**COLIN** Look Shelley I don't know. Anyhow, you asked me about Greece and I told you. So let's drop it. Let's leave it at that.

**SHELLEY** But Colin...

**COLIN** And not a word. Not a word to no bugger. I told you 'cos you're my friend. If you can't handle it fair enough, but mum's the word.

**SHELLEY** Oh Col.

**COLIN** Leave it. And I can tell you something else an' all.

**SHELLEY** What?

**COLIN** I don't want to go back to school.

**SHELLEY** Well we all knows that.

**COLIN** Well I might just not.

**SHELLEY** Don't talk daft. You're chicken shit. You'll never leave.

*COLIN gets up to go.*

**COLIN** Wanna bet? Just watch me. *(He goes.)*

**SHELLEY** Colin where you going? *(She follows him.)* Look I'm sorry. I shan't say a word. It's beyond me but I shan't say nothing. Colin! Colin!

*She runs after him. The sounds of the crashing sea, almost a storm, fill the air as the light dims to grey. The storm passes and the magic flute fills the air. The light rises on a brighter day and COLIN is in the sand dunes.*

**COLIN**   Sun's come out. Come out for the last Sunday The final day of ritual. School starts Wednesday. There's nothing for me here in Swansea.

*MAM and DAD enter.*

**DAD**   Colin are you up them bastard dunes? I'll frigging kill you.

**MAM**   Hold on Dad. Leave it now.

**DAD**   Colin! Colin! There you are. In them bastard dunes. What you bastard playing at you little bastard?

**MAM**   Dad stop it. Not like that.

**DAD**   I'll wring his bastard neck.

**MAM**   Colin! Colin! What's your game? What's all this then?

**COLIN**   Shelley?

**MAM**   Yes Shelley. Shelley told us.

**COLIN**   Shelley … told you?

**MAM**   Yes! We can't believe it.

**COLIN**   I can't believe she told you.

**DAD**   You've got to go.

**MAM**   You gotta go back to school.

**COLIN**   Oh that! *(A pause.)* Why?

**DAD**   Look son we been over all this. You needs your A's. You needs something down on paper. Something substantial.

**MAM**   Dad's right Colin.

**DAD**   Look son, I'm sorry I shouted. But I'm not having you selling cars.

**COLIN**     I won't Dad. I'm going to be a painter.

**DAD**     Oh that bastard crap again.

**MAM**     Look Colin what d 'you reckon you're going to do? I mean come Wednesday what are you going to do? It'll be alright for a few days and then you'll get bored. You can't mope about the house all day long.

**COLIN**     I won't. Come Wednesday I'm going away. I am Mam.

**DAD**     And where you gonna go? Live in some hippie pigging commune?

**COLIN**     I'll get a job. Start my life. My adult life.

**MAM**     Don't talk soft. You're too young to be an adult.

**COLIN**     I'm not Mam. There's things.

**MAM**     What things?

**COLIN**     Dunno. Things I can't explain yet. Things inside me. Give me time and I'll be able to tell you.

**DAD**     How much time?

**MAM**     What things?

**COLIN**     I can't say no more. Not at the moment. Things.

**DAD**     You're not right Colin.

**MAM**     Colin you're acting all soft.

**COLIN**     I'm sorry. That's the way it is. Things.

**MAM**     So your mind's made up?

**COLIN**     Yes.

**MAM**     Well you're a cheeky little bastard that's for sure.

**DAD**   Mam!

**MAM**   Well I took him to bleeding Greece. Cost me a packet. We had a deal. We had a bargain.

**COLIN**   You blackmailed me Mam. We had a good time. Trip was a success.

**MAM**   That's not the point. We made an arrangement. Cost me good money.

**COLIN**   Alright, if that's the way you sees things, I'll let you have it back. When I start working.

**MAM**   I don't mean that.

**COLIN**   No Mam. You can have it. I'm sorry, I'm off.

*COLIN gets up and goes.*

**MAM**   But Colin, Colin, where are you going? Colin!

*He keeps walking.*

**DAD**   Colin! *(He stops.)* Where are you going son? Where you gonna go?

**COLIN**   I'm off in the ocean. I'm gonna surf with the waves.

*He goes.*

**MAM**   We don't mean that. That's not what we mean. We mean where you going?

*A pause. DAD puts his arm around her. For once MAM looks like she might break. The flute plays, the light fades and the gulls cry out. The light rises on COLIN sitting in the dunes. He is sketching and listening to music on his Walkman. After a few moments, a boy, JAMES, walks into the dunes. He wears a back-pack and is listening to music on his Walkman. COLIN continues sketching.*

*JAMES notices COLIN and stops. He wanders back and forth a few times and cruises COLIN. COLIN behaves innocently and only looks up once. Eventually JAMES braves it and sits near COLIN. After a few moments he moves in closer, then closer still. A pause. Finally COLIN looks up at JAMES. They stare at each other. JAMES smiles. COLIN grins back. JAMES mouths "hello". COLIN does the same. JAMES takes off his Walkman and shakes COLIN's hand.*

**JAMES**   Hi. I'm James.

*COLIN takes off his Walkman.*

**COLIN**   I'm sorry?

**JAMES**   My name's James. How are you?

**COLIN**   Hello. I'm Colin. Very well, thanks. Alright?

**JAMES**   Yes. *(A pause.)* Beach is quiet today.

**COLIN**   Yeah. End of the season. Some schools went back yesterday. The rest tomorrow. It's quiet today. *(A pause.)* What about you?

**JAMES**   Sorry?

**COLIN**   School?

**JAMES**   Oh, yes. Next Monday.

**COLIN**   How come?

**JAMES**   I go away to school.

**COLIN**   Oh, I see. That's why you talk all poncey.

**JAMES**   Ha! And you?

**COLIN**   Swansea through and through.

**JAMES**   I meant school.

**COLIN**   Oh tomorrow. We goes back tomorrow. But

I'm not going.

**JAMES** Special leave?

**COLIN** Just leaving. I'm not going back at all.

**JAMES** Really? Jammy sod.

**COLIN** Yes I'm off me. Off away. It's second year of A's. But I hates it. Are you doing A's?

**JAMES** Next summer. Where are you going?

**COLIN** I bought a ticket. I'm off to London. On the Rapide. Eight forty-five tomorrow morning.

**JAMES** Are you on your own? Today?

**COLIN** Yes. Everyone's at work. My brother's back to school. I come down for a final butcher's. Do a bit of sketching.

**JAMES** It's good. You're good. *(A pause.)* A naked man.

**COLIN** Yes.

**JAMES** It looks good. He looks good. Anyone in particular?

**COLIN** Just this bloke. Ari. This Greek bloke. In Greece.

**JAMES** Big cock.

**COLIN** Yes.

**JAMES** It's good. Sexy. You like cocks. *(A silence.)* D'you want a blow-job?

**COLIN** Christ!

**JAMES** D'you?

**COLIN** Where?

**JAMES** Between your legs of course.

**COLIN** Christ! Are you putting me on?

**JAMES** Isn't that what you're after? *(A silence.)* Haven't you seen them?

**COLIN** What?

**JAMES** The blokes. Down here. In the dunes.

**COLIN** Where?

**JAMES** Down there. There's always some blokes down there. At it. In the dunes.

**COLIN** Never? But I comes here all the time. I'm always down here.

**JAMES** You've got your eyes closed. Well d 'you want this blow-job or not?

**COLIN** Oh Christ. Christ Ari it's my chance all over again.

**JAMES** Sorry?

**COLIN** Well yes. Yes I do.

**JAMES** Come on then. Over here.

*JAMES goes behind a higher dune covered in bush, where he is hidden from the waist down. COLIN follows.*

**JAMES** Don't be shy.

*JAMES rubs COLIN's crotch.*

**COLIN** I'm getting an hard-on.

**JAMES** That's the idea.

**COLIN** You're getting my cock out.

**JAMES** That's right.

**COLIN**   I think I might ejaculate immediately.

**JAMES**   Relax. Don't be so tense. It's beautiful.

**COLIN**   What is?

**JAMES**   Your cock.

*JAMES drop to his knees and disappears from sight.*

**COLIN**   Oh. Nice. Very nice. Oh that's lovely. Not at all toothy. This is what I've been waiting for. Worth the waiting. This is, eh? Oh my. It's beautiful. Really beautiful. I'm going away. Far away. On the Rapide. Very far to London. Far away. I'm going away. I'm going. I'm going. I'm going. *(COLIN hears voices calling in his head, MAM. DAD, SHELLEY, ARI. They shout out: "Colin! Colin! Colin where are you? Where are you Colin! Colin! Colin!")* I'm going. I'm going to come. *(The voices continue.)* I'm coming. I'm coming. It's alright I'm coming. I'm coming! I'm coming out. Out. Out. Out. *(The voice stops. He screams. He is short of breath. He looks down.)* He's gone. James! He's gone. I come on my own. I had an orgasm all on my own. Without touching myself. He's gone. Quite gone. I'm off then. Off down the ocean. My very last dip. I'm going in the sea.

*He takes of his clothes and rushing off through the dunes we see his bare bum.*

*He yells out.*

**COLIN**   I'm off to London! I'll swim to London!

*The light fades to black.*

# ACT TWO

*The attic floor of an old derelict warehouse in East London. Large semicircular windows overlook decrepit factories and other derelict buildings. Down below there is a railway line and the rattle of trains can be heard from time to time. Also close by is the sound of church bells and a clock chiming every fifteen minutes. Every evening a mullah chants the call to prayer at the neighbouring moslem temple.*

*This is COLIN's home. Bare floorboards and brick walls. In one corner a double bed covered with an old quilt. A large sofa draped in indian cloth. An old fifties fridge, a cooking ring, a lovely old wooden table and kitchen chairs. A T.V. And stereo. A telephone. An open rail for hanging clothes. The overall effect is attractive yet meagre.*

*One area is dominated by a large easel and canvas. A door to the bathroom. Another door to the stairway down to the street. A neighbour below practises his saxophone.*

*As the lights rise we are able to see the room from the mixture of moonlight and amber street lamps outside the circular windows. A train passes.*

*The telephone is ringing. The door to the stairs opens and COLIN enters followed by JAMES. They both wear leather jackets, denim jeans, Dr. Martens. They enter in the half-light and COLIN swerves towards the phone. It stops as he reaches it. He switches on a bedside lamp.*

*JAMES hovers in the doorway.*

**JAMES**   Might be time to invest in an answer machine? I'm told they're all the rage.

*COLIN switches on the kettle in the kitchen area.*

**COLIN**   Ha. Well come in then. Don't stop by there.

**JAMES**   No.

*James closes the door but remains standing in the same place.*

**COLIN**   Cup of tea?

**JAMES**   Yes. Thanks.

**COLIN**   Herbal or regular?

**JAMES**   Camomile?

**COLIN**   No sooner said. *(COLIN prepares the tea.)* Christ come in. Come in. You looks soft over by there.

**JAMES**   Sorry.

*JAMES enters.*

**COLIN**   Now you're the shy one. Last time we met it was me.

**JAMES**   I know. It's stupid isn't it?

**COLIN**   Sit down for Christ's sake. Take your jacket off. Relax.

**JAMES**   What's that music? *(The saxophone stops.)* I don't believe it. It's stopped.

**COLIN**   That's Max. He's very sensitive to criticism.

**JAMES**   I wasn't criticising.

**COLIN**   I'm teasing. That was a coincidence. You know. The music stopping like that. A coincidence. Remember them? Like us. Meeting tonight.

**JAMES**   Indeed.

**COLIN**   That's Max on his sax. My neighbour. Downstairs. Plays in a band.

**JAMES**   It's great. This place.

**COLIN**   Thankyou.

**JAMES**   To have your own place. And in this part of London.

**COLIN**   Well, the East End isn't everyone's notion of an holiday. But I like it. This'll sound daft. But it reminds me of Swansea. Roots. It's friendly over here. And less of an hassle.

**JAMES**   How long have you lived here?

**COLIN**   Nearly six months. Tea.

**JAMES**   Thankyou.

**COLIN**   When I first come up, that was September. Nearly four years ago. It's nearly four years since we met.

**JAMES**   Well, three years eleven months. And a bit.

**COLIN**   Pedantic. When I first come up. I felt like an arsehole. A stupid Welsh arsehole. I wanted to go straight back. I went to this guest house. In Victoria. A rip-off place. Then I got this cupboard. Cupboard in Earls Court. 63, Barkston Gardens. Top bell. Twenty of us to one bath. It was really shitty. Kilburn Battersea Brixton Camberwell. Then ... I got this place. Right next to Brick Lane.

**JAMES**   It's fierce. And you're painting.

**COLIN**  When I can. Shall I put some music on?

**JAMES**  No. No it's nice. I like the quiet. It's nice to talk. *(A train rumbles past sounding a loud signal.)* Every time I make a comment about the sounds round here, something happens.

**COLIN**  That's the eleven-twenty.

*JAMES gets up and looks out of the window.*

**JAMES**  Jesus! This is how I imagine New York.

**COLIN**  Wouldn't know about that.

*COLIN opens the window. JAMES sits up on the window ledge.*

**JAMES**  This is stunning. City air.

**COLIN**  What about you?

**JAMES**  What?

**COLIN**  What have you been up to? Since I saw you. In the dunes. Look I'm sorry.

**JAMES**  No, I'm sorry. I'm the one should apologise. I was really embarrassed when I saw you tonight. I saw you and I thought "He's cute, really cute bloke. I'll check him out." And you hadn't seen me. And I was staring at you and I thought "Yeah he's really cute. I'll go and stand opposite him." And then I thought "Wait a minute, I know him. Where from? I'm sure I know him. I think I met him in Swansea". And then I remembered. I thought "Oh fuck I've got to get out of here." Then I thought "That's stupid. I'll just avoid him." And then you came up to me.

**COLIN**  Well that's really funny 'cos I noticed you and I recognized you straight away. Immediately I knew you. And I felt really stupid. For what I'd done. And I just wanted to come and say sorry. And to thank you.

**JAMES**  Thank me?

**COLIN**  And I came up to you and the look on your face was so shocked I couldn't say nothing. 'Cept hello.

**JAMES**  I'm glad you did. But I'm the one to be sorry. Doing a bunk like that.

**COLIN**  No it was me. Screaming my tits off in the dunes.

**JAMES**  I was terrified. I was frightened someone might come. The police or something. So I legged it.

**COLIN**  I know. I was an arsehole. It was my first you see. So I wanted to thank you. First time any bloke.

**JAMES**  Ever?

**COLIN**  Yes.

**JAMES**  But not your last?

**COLIN**  Happily, there've been a few since.

**JAMES**  But no boyfriends?

**COLIN**  Well. There was this... there was this bloke lasted three days. Then this other one three and a half weeks. Well three weeks two and a half days actually. D'you reckon they count?

**JAMES**  Don't reckon they do.

**COLIN**  No. Sick isn't it? Still I don't care. I got this place. I got away from Swansea. I'm painting. And at least I know it's boys I want. Anyway what about you? What about your studies? University?

**JAMES**  A 2:1.

**COLIN**  Bloody hell that's fucking brilliant!

**JAMES** Not outstanding. But good-ish.

**COLIN** Come on, it's genius. And now?

**JAMES** We'll see. I'm sorry. This is going to sound awful, but what's your name?

**COLIN** Colin. You're James.

**JAMES** You see, you're the brilliant one.

**COLIN** Fuck off.

**JAMES** I'm sincere.

**COLIN** Fuck off!

**JAMES** Just testing.

**COLIN** For what?

**JAMES** Sense of humour.

**COLIN** Satisfied?

**JAMES** For starters. So what do you do?

**COLIN** Excuse me?

**JAMES** Work, I mean. I mean do you work?

**COLIN** Just testing.

**JAMES** Cheeky.

**COLIN** Worked in a factory. Worked in a shoe shop. Now I'm waiting tables. Actually, I'm trying to get a job in an art supply shop. But they're harder to get in. Discounts all round.

*JAMES goes to look at COLIN's easel.*

**JAMES** You're good. You're talented.

**COLIN** Dunno.

**JAMES** Come on. Don't be so modest. You are. I

remember your drawing. Of that bloke. He was Greek.

**COLIN**   That's right. Ari. He keeps writing. He's planning to come over this Autumn.

**JAMES**   I had a wank.

**COLIN**   When?

**JAMES**   That night. In bed.

**COLIN**   Did you?

**JAMES**   I thought about that drawing – of Ari, and I started getting horny. Then I thought about you. And I had a wank.

**COLIN**   Good. I'm flattered. Both as an artist and a bloke.

*A pause. They kiss. They break away, a little embarrassed.*

**JAMES**   What about you?

**COLIN**   What?

**JAMES**   Did you go to Art school?

**COLIN**   A year and a half at Camberwell. Then I left. It wasn't for me. D'you want to stay the night?

**JAMES**   I can't. I'm sorry. I'm not being funny. I'm staying with these friends. In South Ken.

**COLIN**   There's crachach.

**JAMES**   I'll have to get back. Catch the last tube.

**COLIN**   You best be going. District Line. Get it from Aldgate East. Two minutes away.

**JAMES**   I'm sorry. I'm not being funny.

**COLIN**   Don't be soft. What did you read at University.

**JAMES**   English.

**COLIN**   English. Come 'ere.

*They kiss again.*

**JAMES**   I'm going back to Swansea for a bit. Can I call you? See you when I get back?

**COLIN**   Course you can. *(COLIN writes down his telephone number.)* Call me when you want.

**JAMES**   I will. I'll call you when I want. *(He picks up his jacket and goes to the doorway. The saxophone starts up.)* Your Max has got interesting timing.

**COLIN**   He's sensitive to moods.

**JAMES**   Colin?

**COLIN**   Yes?

**JAMES**   I'm sorry. I'm sorry I ran out on you. Before. I'm not doing the same now.

**COLIN**   See you later.

*The door closes and COLIN is alone. He stands in the middle of the room for a minute listening to the saxophone. A train rumbles past. He closes the window.*

*He goes to his easel and looks at his painting. He picks up a brush and palette, turns a desk light onto the easel and starts to paint. The sound of the saxophone fills the room and the lights fade until only the half-light from outside shines in on COLIN painting and then to nothing.*

*The saxophone fades and the lights come up on the room early afternoon. COLIN opens a window and throws a latchkey on a string (like a baby parachute) to the street below, then opens the door to the stairway and leaves it ajar. He puts on the kettle. After a few moments there is a tapping on the door.*

**COLIN** Come in.

*SHELLEY enters.*

**SHELLEY** Blimey them stairs babes. I'm getting fat. Gi's a look at you.

*They hug. She hands him the latchkey on a string.*

**SHELLEY** You looks great.

**COLIN** You look gorgeous. How are you?

*They hug again.*

**COLIN** Come in. Come in.

**SHELLEY** Jesus! There's unusual.

**COLIN** Come in Shell. Don't look so shell-shocked.

**SHELLEY** No. It's lovely. I mean it's London isn't it? You lives in London.

**COLIN** D'you want some tea?

**SHELLEY** Ta.

**COLIN** Herbal or regular?

**SHELLEY** What?

**COLIN** PG Tips it is.

**SHELLEY** Ta. One and a half sugars. God I'm getting fat.

**COLIN** You're not pregnant are you Shell?

**SHELLEY** Give over. I left my suitcase in the hall downstairs. That's alright isn't it?

**COLIN** Yes. It'll be safe.

**SHELLEY** I can't stop long.

**COLIN** So what's this course you're doing?

**SHELLEY** Oh, its two days. We starts tomorrow. At this big hotel in Hammersmith. It's "Management Training." Boots have hired all these rooms. If I get on well I'll be Under Manager's Assistant.

**COLIN** Sounds good.

**SHELLEY** Big deal.

**COLIN** Come on Shell. You've done well for yourself. Remember how scared you were? First day of work.

**SHELLEY** I got a taxi from Paddington. But I can't stop long. I'll get another one to Hammersmith.

**COLIN** Bloody hell. You're flush.

**SHELLEY** Expenses. All down to expenses. They've moved your Mam to C.D.'s. But she's fed up.

**COLIN** Yeah. She keeps on about it on the phone.

**SHELLEY** Colin, I've got something to tell you. It's Mam. She died. Died six weeks ago.

**COLIN** Shelley. I'm sorry. *(He goes to her and hugs her.)* Shelley. I'm sorry.

**SHELLEY** Oh Col. It was pathetic to watch her. Poor little mite. She never done no harm. *(They hug again.)* No It's alright. It's best really. Her life was miserable. She's better off out of it.

**COLIN** And you nursed her?

**SHELLEY** Yeah. That was the best part. A real privilege. Helped us get close.

**COLIN** But I didn't know. No one said.

**SHELLEY** My fault. I wanted to tell you myself. And I knew I'd be coming up.

**COLIN** Shelley, I'm sorry.

**SHELLEY** Where's this bleeding tea?

*He makes the tea.*

**COLIN** So you're living on your tod an' all then?

**SHELLEY** Yeah. We're a right pair aren't we? Few years ago we was kids. Now look at us.

**COLIN** What d'you reckon we are now then?

**SHELLEY** Big kids. Big soft kids. Bigger ones anyhow.

**COLIN** Tea.

**SHELLEY** Ta. I got a bloke. Oh Colin. He's gorgeous. His name's Derek. And he's really good to me. He's a real gent. He'd like to marry me. He keeps asking. But I says "Don't be soft." I'm too young see. I want to do things. Do things with my life. I don't want my life revolving round no bloke. I wants a career. But he's gorgeous, he is Col. And he was great when Mam died. He used to sit with her. Sit with her for hours. Hours on end. Tell her stories and jokes and stuff. I often used to wonder. Wonder who the bloody hell he was dating. Me or Mam.

**COLIN** That's brilliant, Shell. I'm happy for you. What does he do?

**SHELLEY** He's Under Manager at Boots.

**COLIN** Never! Nepotism eh?

**SHELLEY** Derek persuaded me to do the course. Pushed me in the right direction. Well I'm glad. I'm doing what I want to be doing. *(A pause.)* What about you?

**COLIN** What?

**SHELLEY** Got a boyfriend?

**COLIN** Not exactly.

**SHELLEY** What about your painting?

**COLIN** Doing my best.

**SHELLEY** Then you'll do it. I knows you. You're a lad who knows what he wants. Can I have a butcher's?

**COLIN** Course.

*She goes to his easel.*

**SHELLEY** God it's brilliant, Col. You cowing brilliant babes.

**COLIN** I sold a painting last week. £500.

**SHELLEY** Jesus – our Colin! So what about the boys then? Spill the beans. Where's all the boys in your life?

**COLIN** Don't ask.

**SHELLEY** Go on.

**COLIN** There's tons of bars round here. Gay bars. In this neighbourhood. You can walk to them or a short bus ride, but oh, I don't know.

**SHELLEY** What?

**COLIN** Well you go to a bar and they're either in clumps, that's the worst, little gangs of them, they think they're it; they just look like they're making fun of everyone, looking down their noses and sending people up, or they're alone. Totally alone. And they're either desperate and keep staring desperately at anyone who comes by or they act all cool and don't look at no-one all night long. They got a word for it up here – attitude. They calls it "attitude". "He's got a real attitude problem. Don't give me attitude."

**SHELLEY** Tell me about it. Straight blokes are no better. They just want to get poked. A girl can't go out on the town for a giggle. She's got to be a slag. She can't have a few drinks too many. She got to be a drunken slag. Some of them blokes get so pissed they can't stand up. They vomiting everywhere and they looks like they're on the edge of a coma. It's pathetic. They the drunken slags, I can tell you.

*A mullah chants in the distance. Shelley stares.*

**COLIN** Call to prayer. It's the Moslem temple.

**SHELLEY** Jesus, it's a funny neighbourhood this.

**COLIN** There is this bloke actually.

**SHELLEY** Go on.

**COLIN** Seen him a couple of times. Well twice actually. Two times. Well one and a half. But ...

**SHELLEY** Yeah?

**COLIN** Well he's great. Really nice. And cute. Yes he's cute. And you'll never guess?

**SHELLEY** What?

**COLIN** He comes from Swansea.

**SHELLEY** Never? *(The saxophone starts up.)* What the hell?

**COLIN** My neighbour downstairs. He's a musician.

**SHELLEY** Blimey. There's different. What's his name?

**COLIN** Max.

**SHELLEY** Max. Don't know no Maxes in Swansea.

**COLIN** Oh no, no. Max is my neighbour. His name's James.

**SHELLEY** James what? Bond?

**COLIN** Don't know his surname.

**SHELLEY** First name terms only. Have you? Have you ... done it?

**COLIN** Shellshocked you never change. You'll never alter.

**SHELLEY** Don't say that

**COLIN** You're a filthy cow.

**SHELLEY** Cheeky bastard. Well have you?

**COLIN** Not really.

**SHELLEY** What does that mean?

**COLIN** No. No. We haven't.

**SHELLEY** But you wants to?

**COLIN** Desperately. Oh Shelley he's great. Gorgeous he is. I'm desperate to do it with him.

**SHELLEY** But?

**COLIN** Well, I'd like a relationship. Some sort of structure.

**SHELLEY** You don't want to be a tart?

**COLIN** No I don't.

**SHELLEY** Poor Colin. You always wants what's hardest in life.

**COLIN** Is that what you think?

**SHELLEY** Yeah.

**COLIN** You just said I was lad who knows what he wants.

**SHELLEY** You are. You wants what's hardest.

**COLIN** What?

**SHELLEY** Art. Love. Romance. The lot. You're an idealist. I think that's the word. I'm trying to go to the library. Read up. Don't look put out. I said you was an idealist, not a wanker.

**COLIN** Makes me feel like a wanker.

**SHELLEY** Come on, stop feeling sorry for yourself. Christ Col, I gotta go. We got this dinner tonight. At the hotel. I got to get over there. Mousse my hair. Fix that mascara.

**COLIN** Sounds like you're hunting.

**SHELLEY** It's not every night a Swansea girl finds herself up in London.

**COLIN** You be careful Shell.

**SHELLEY** Don't talk soft. I can handle myself. Will I get a taxi on the street?

**COLIN** Easy.

**SHELLEY** I loves that music. It's sexy it is.

**COLIN** You're in a horny mood I can tell.

**SHELLEY** Come here you soft bastard. Give us a cuddle.

*They hug.*

**COLIN** Good luck tomorrow.

**SHELLEY** Under Manager's Bleeding Assistant. I'm going to run Boots me. Gonna be Bessy Bossy Boots herself.

*She goes.*

*COLIN goes and stands by the telephone for a few moments. He goes to his bed and lies down. The saxophone fills the room. The lights fade to night-light from the street.*

*The saxophone fades and the lights come up in the room. It is late evening and the light is dimming outside. The bedside lamp is on. The nearby church clock chimes nine.*

*JAMES and COLIN are sitting at the kitchen table. They have finished eating pizzas. The cartons are lying around. They are drinking red wine and are a little merry.*

**COLIN**  I should've cooked you my favourite.

**JAMES**  What's that?

**COLIN**  Mashed potatoes cheese top.

**JAMES**  You working class boys have got strange tastes.

**COLIN**  Big snob. What's your favourite then?

**JAMES**  Coq au vin. *(He rubs the wine bottle, saucily.)*

**COLIN**  Don't be dirty.

**JAMES**  Gravalax.

**COLIN**  Don't show off.

**JAMES**  No it is. My favourite. It's a Scandinavian salmon. Marinated.

**COLIN**  Just 'cos you comes from Derwen Fawr there's no need to get so poncey. *(JAMES kisses COLIN.)* I'm glad you phoned. I didn't think you would.

**JAMES**  Told you I wasn't running out.

**COLIN**  How was Swansea? You haven't really said.

**JAMES**  Wet. Kept pissing down.

**COLIN**  Did you go down the dunes?

**JAMES**  Only to look for you.

**COLIN**  Don't be soft.

**JAMES** I can stay tonight. That is if you want me to.

**COLIN** 'Course. *(A pause.)* Have you ever had a boyfriend?

**JAMES** Steady? Involved?

**COLIN** Yes.

**JAMES** No way.

**COLIN** Don't you want to?

**JAMES** Are you getting heavy?

**COLIN** Whoops.

**JAMES** I'm teasing. No I've never had a boyfriend. Well there was this other boy, at school. I had a huge crush on him. Blonde curly hair. Played rugby. Flyhalf. God he was horny. And we used to have great sex. Went on for months. Then one day he just cut me off. Cut me dead. Wouldn't even talk to me. He was older. Older than me. And I think he was frightened that word had got out. That a rumour might be circulating. And he got paranoid. That's what it's like at school. Pathetic isn't it?

**COLIN** Yes. It's pathetic. Were you very hurt?

**JAMES** It fucked me up completely. For about a year. And then I thought "Fuck it. What's the point of all this? Moping about because of some douche-bag. Forget him." So I did. Least I pretended I did. Then he left school. And that made it all much easier.

**COLIN** Let's go and lie down.

**JAMES** Thanks for the pizza.

**COLIN** Thank Pizza Express.

*They get up. COLIN throws the pizza cartons away.*

**JAMES** Shall I bring the wine?

**COLIN**  Please.

*A train rumbles by.*

**JAMES**  Don't they aggravate you? Those fucking trains.

**COLIN**  They soothe me. It's life. Motion. Makes me feel less lonely.

**JAMES**  Are you lonely?

**COLIN**  Sometimes. Isn't everyone?

**JAMES**  Never really thought about it. Well no. I'm not. Not so far. Unhappy sometimes. Like when I lost the Rugby tackle. But lonely ...

**COLIN**  I have a lot of spare time. To myself, Sometimes I get lonely.

**JAMES**  What about your family? You're close to them. I'm not. I'm not really close to anyone. Not even my family. I've always lived away from home. As long as I can remember.

**COLIN**  I'm sorry.

**JAMES**  Don't be.

**COLIN**  Mam and Dad are coming up next week. First time. Their first visit. And I still haven't been home. Not since I left.

*They lie down on the bed.*

**JAMES**  Why not?

**COLIN**  Pride, I s'pose. I didn't want to go home till I'd achieved something. Till I'd done things.

**JAMES**  But you have. You've got your own place. You make your own money. You're independent.

**COLIN**    S'pose.

**JAMES**    Independent.

**COLIN**    My Dad still sends me money. Secretly. He's soft like that.

**JAMES**    Yes, but you're working.

**COLIN**    Well you're brainy. A 2:1.

**JAMES**    Bullshit. I'm going through the system. Going through the hoops. You escaped. You're the one that got away. You're the one who'll do great things.

**COLIN**    Bullshit.

*Max starts playing.*

**JAMES**    He's great your neighbour. Brilliant at setting the mood. *(JAMES leans over and kisses COLIN.)* God you're beautiful. Incredible eyes.

**COLIN**    Give over. I'm a mongrel me.

**JAMES**    A mongrel pup.

**COLIN**    Why do you reckon?

**JAMES**    Why, what?

**COLIN**    We turn out gay. One way or the other.

**JAMES**    Please, don't go all existentialist on me.

**COLIN**    No. I'm serious.

**JAMES**    Who isn't?

**COLIN**    Dunno.

**JAMES**    Christ Colin don't look so glum. What difference does it make? What difference does it make who we sleep with? That's private. It's a private matter. Who we fuck with is our own affair. Individual choice. In every other respect we're just as boring as everyone else.

**COLIN** Just as pretty.

*COLIN pecks JAMES.*

**JAMES** Just as horny.

*JAMES kisses COLIN.*

**COLIN** Just as talented.

**JAMES** Just as useless.

**COLIN** Just as hard-working.

**JAMES** As indolent.

**COLIN** As curious.

**JAMES** Bored.

**COLIN** Catholic.

**JAMES** Bored now, bye.

*He slaps COLIN's arse. A pause. The saxophone stops playing. JAMES pours more wine. COLIN sits up.*

**COLIN** James?

**JAMES** Colin?

**COLIN** James?

**JAMES** Colin?

**COLIN** James I don't know how to put this.

**JAMES** Don't tell me. You're having another man's baby. I knew you were a deep one. Don't worry darling I'll adopt.

**COLIN** Be serious. I'm serious. Why can't you be serious?

**JAMES** Fuck it, I'm sorry. Just a joke.

**COLIN** No I'm sorry. Forget it. It's me. It's just that

I'm trying to say something and I don't know how. I don't want to cause offence.

**JAMES** Try me.

**COLIN** Well you see the thing is ... it's like this ... oh fuck it. Fuck it. I'm trying to say. Just before I came to London. Same time I first met you. That's when I knew. Knew I was gay.

**JAMES** Colin you are getting heavy.

**COLIN** And I'm happy that I knows that. What I mean is I'm happy I'm gay. A lot of people assume gay people must be unhappy 'cos they're not what others think of as normal. But I'm happy. Happy in my knowledge. Happy in myself.

**JAMES** Good Colin good.

**COLIN** Right! So the thing is I like sex. Quite a lot of sex actually. *(He pecks JAMES.)* But I don't like cruising. What I want is someone I can have sex with regularly. A friend. Someone who's my friend. Who I can sleep with. Nothing heavy like. Just take it as it comes. Take it at a normal pace. But regular sex with the same person.

**JAMES** Is that all? Listen, that's fine by me. I reckon we're after the same thing. Regular sex with a good mate.

**COLIN** Yes.

**JAMES** So that's settled then. Can I borrow a toothbrush?

**COLIN** I'm afraid there's more.

**JAMES** Fuck!

**COLIN** I took the AIDS Test. The HIV test. The Antibody test.

**JAMES** Fuck me. You're a brave fool. And you're trying to tell me?

**COLIN** Yes.

**JAMES** You're trying to tell me you're HIV?

**COLIN** No. Oh no. No I'm sorry. I'm trying to tell you I'm not.

**JAMES** You stupid sod. I'm really pleased for you Colin. I could never take that creepy test. Idea scares the shit out of me.

**COLIN** That's the problem.

**JAMES** What do you mean?

**COLIN** Well the problem is ... whoever I'm sleeping with, whoever's my partner, I want to know. I want to know their status. I want to know what I'm up against.

**JAMES** What?

**COLIN** I want to know, if I'm sleeping with someone regular, whether they're HIV or not.

**JAMES** Marvellous darling. Absolutely fucking marvellous. He wants me to take the test. The creepola test. So I take the test and I fail and we're fucked and I'm completely fucked. Great. Where do I sign?

**COLIN** Don't be soft. For one thing you'll probably test negative. And even if you didn't I'd stand by you.

**JAMES** Fuck off!

**COLIN** I mean it. I've thought a lot about this. In respect to you. To us.

**JAMES** How could you? We've only met twice. And

then briefly.

**COLIN**   Twice before. But that last time. I knew I liked you.

**JAMES**   And on the strength of that you took the test?

**COLIN**   Not exactly no. I've been mulling it over for a while. Anyhow I could just as easily have tested positive. And the situation would have been the same.

**JAMES**   Only different.

**COLIN**   I mean I wouldn't want to start up something if I was positive without telling the other person.

**JAMES**   But you're not positive. And you're not prepared to start anything before vetting all potential candidates.

**COLIN**   I just want to know where I stand

**JAMES**   Why? A condom's a condom's a condom.

**COLIN**   You make me out a bastard.

**JAMES**   You are. A cheeky bastard. *(A pause.)* What it comes down to is you're asking me to take the test.

**COLIN**   I'm asking you to consider it.

**JAMES**   No test. No nooky.

**COLIN**   Don't be daft. You can stop over anyhow.

**JAMES**   That story you told me earlier on about your mother and Greece and A levels? It's the same thing. Blackmail.

**COLIN**   That's ridiculous.

**JAMES**   But until we know whether I'm HIV or not we can't be boyfriends.

**COLIN**   I don't know. It's confusing. When you put it like that.

**JAMES**  Well you should have thought about all this before.

**COLIN**  Look I'm sorry.

**JAMES**  So fuck you. You're a cheeky bastard.

*He gets up to go.*

**COLIN**  I'm sorry. I didn't mean to offend you.

*He gets his jacket.*

**JAMES**  I've been sleeping with blokes since I was fourteen. Chances are I am positive. We can't all be little angels like you. So what if I am? What then?

**COLIN**  Well wouldn't it be better to know?

**JAMES**  Oh yes and stick around for full blown AIDS? To be called a PWA. Person With AIDS. My life hasn't even begun. No thank you very much.

**COLIN**  The knowledge isn't going to change anything.

**JAMES**  Ever heard of stress? Suppose the 'knowledge' stresses you out? I'll tell you something Colin you may be negative but you're fucking naive.

*JAMES leaves, slamming the door. Max starts playing.*

**COLIN**  James don't go. Please. (*COLIN goes to the door and opens it, shouts down the stairs.*) Please James. I'm sorry. Please. (*He opens the window onto the street and shouts out.*) James! I'm sorry. I'm an arsehole. Forgive me. I'm a stupid Welsh arsehole. I'm sorry.

*The saxophone floods through the room and the lights fade. The lights come up and COLIN is tidying the room. A tap on the door which is ajar.*

*MAM enters.*

**MAM** Jesus them stairs Col! Murder for my varicose. Let's have a look. Look at you. You've lost weight. You're not eating properly. Let's have a look. Come by 'ere you monkey. (*He goes to her. They embrace.*) You big soft kid. You looks wonderful boy. God I missed you.

**COLIN** I miss you too Mam. You look well.

**MAM** Well I chucked Boots. I've finally done it. Handed in my notice last Saturday. Finish at the end of the month.

**COLIN** That's brilliant. But what you going to do?

**MAM** Excuse me but sweet F.A. I've had enough of the sodding lot of it. I'm going to be a lady of leisure. Shelley's doing well. Come through that Management training with flying colours. In fact she done so well they making her an Assistant Manager. That's one up from Under Manager's Assistant and one below Under Manager theyself. And she's finished with Derek. Said he was interfering. Interfering with the progress of her career.

**COLIN** Cheeky tart.

**MAM** But me – they puts me on C.D.s and I get all these little punks, green eyes and orange hair, asking for The Cure, all day long. I says to them "If you wants the cure you'd better go to the pharmacy counter. This is C bleeding D's. Cheeky beggars they complains. Complains about the way I talks to them. I been ticked off by management three times. I thought "Oh I'm off, I don't need this."

**COLIN** Oh Mam!

**MAM**  I left Dad in Hamleys.

**COLIN**  How come?

**MAM**  We got a surprise for you.

**COLIN**  Mam I'm too old for toys.

**MAM**  Not for you. For someone else. A little visitor.

**COLIN**  What?

**MAM**  Anyhow don't go on. It's a surprise. You'll spoil things. He'll be here soon. Anyhow gives us a chance. For a bit of a natter. Aren't you going to offer me something?

**COLIN**  Cup of tea?

**MAM**  No I fancies something stronger. Got any gin?

**COLIN**  Sorry Mam I haven't. Got some beer.

**MAM**  Go on. That'll do.

*COLIN gets two beers. They sit down. A train rumbles past.*

**MAM**  What's that?

**COLIN**  The 12.45.

**MAM**  The what?

**COLIN**  Trains. It's the railway line.

**MAM**  It's a funny place this Col. A funny neighbourhood. The taxi driver says "Are you sure? Sure you got the right address?" I says "Yes, my son lives by 'ere." He goes "I hopes so madam, 'cos there's no-one lives down 'ere but a lot of rats and a few Pakkies." I says "You cheeky beggar, don't be racist." I didn't give him no tip.

**COLIN**  Good for you.

**MAM** But it is a funny place mind Col.

**COLIN** So what d 'you think of the flat?

**MAM** Interesting. Open plan. And you're still painting?

**COLIN** Yeah.

**MAM** Good. I'm pleased. You'd set your heart on it. I'm pleased for you.

**COLIN** How's Keith?

**MAM** Oh he's great. He scored 38 last season.

**COLIN** That's good innit?

**MAM** GOOD? Bleeding brilliant! He's an ace little shooter. He says hello.

**COLIN** Right.

*A pause.*

**MAM** Go on then. Tell me. Tell me about your life. What you does. Who your friends are.

**COLIN** Well it's not so easy is it? I mean it's different. It's all so different from Swansea. I got a new job.

**MAM** Never?

**COLIN** Working in an Art Supply shop. In the West End.

**MAM** That's great boy. And what about your social life? London friendly is it?

**COLIN** Mam?

*A pause.*

**MAM** Yes love?

**COLIN** Mam there's something I've got to tell you.

**MAM** Fire away.

**COLIN** Something I've been wanting to tell you for a while.

**MAM** Well here I am.

**COLIN** Mam?

**MAM** Yes? *(A pause)* What's the matter love? You're not in no trouble?

**COLIN** No.

**MAM** It's not money is it? 'Cos if it is, don't be afraid to ask your father.

**COLIN** No Mam.

**MAM** I'll ask him for you.

**COLIN** No Mam!

**MAM** It's not a girl Col? You haven't put a girl in the club?

**COLIN** Mam you're racing.

**MAM** Well go on then. Tell us.

**COLIN** Mam, I'm gay.

*A long pause. Finally MAM smiles. She starts to laugh. She stops. Another pause.*

**MAM** Colin, I'm sorry. I don't follow.

**COLIN** I'm gay, Mam. Gay.

**MAM** Oh buggerations. You means poofter gay?

**COLIN** Don't put it like that Mam but yes.

**MAM** Jesus, I don't fucking believe it.

**COLIN** Mam don't swear.

**MAM** Your father said this.

**COLIN** What?

**MAM** Your father said this was a possibility. He said to me "I reckon our Colin might be gay." I said "Homo?"

**COLIN** Well he was right, Mam.

**MAM** You can't be, Colin. What's the matter with you?

**COLIN** There's nothing the matter.

**MAM** It's my fault innit? It's bleeding well my fault. I done something wrong. Me and your father. Rowing in front of you. We should've hidden things.

**COLIN** No, Mam, no. That's been the best. The way you and Dad are is the best, honest it is.

**MAM** Then why, Colin, why? It's not right.

**COLIN** You mean it's wrong?

**MAM** Course it's wrong. It's not normal is it? Look don't get me wrong, Col, I got nothing against them. There's this bloke works in Boots and he's the loveliest bloke he is honest. He's one of the nicest people at work. And there's a couple of lesbians. Work in the stock room. Humping. They're a right laugh. And everyone knows about them and no-one gives a buggers. But you're my boy. It's different innit? Your own flesh and blood.

**COLIN** Why Mam? Why should it be?

**MAM** This is no time to be homo, Colin. I'm sorry "gay". This is not the right time.

**COLIN** I'll hold off for a while then.

**MAM** I mean with AIDS and everything.

**COLIN** AIDS belongs to everyone, Mam. It's not a gay plague.

**MAM** I knows that. I knows that.

**COLIN** I can sleep with a man. I can have sex with a man without getting AIDS.

**MAM** Now Colin, don't be revolting. Don't press things in my face like that. It's disgusting.

**COLIN** It's not, it's normal! It's normal for me!

**MAM** Oh, I'm off. I didn't come up to London to be shouted at by you. You've changed, Colin. You really have. I don't recognise you.

**COLIN** Don't. Don't say that, Mam. I have changed. I've become myself. This is me. Colin. Colin Rhys.

**MAM** And what you gonna do, Colin Rhys? Drift from one encounter to the next? I knows. I knows what it's like.

**COLIN** It's not like that. It doesn't have to be. Being gay is just as boring and just as difficult as being straight or being anything else.

**MAM** Don't be stupid. It's not the same. Your father and me got married. In a Church. We had two kids. Stuck it out when the going got rough.

**COLIN** Did you?

**MAM** What?

**COLIN** Did you always stick it out?

**MAM** What d'you mean?

**COLIN** What about Greece? You and Ari?

**MAM** What are you saying?

**COLIN** Come on Mam, I'm not stupid.

**MAM** I don't like what you're insinuating. Besides which it's none of your business. Your father and me stuck it out.

**COLIN** So what *are* you saying? What's the difference?

**MAM** Between us and homos what pokes everything that moves?

**COLIN** Where d'you get that idea?

**MAM** You're a kid. You wouldn't understand.

**COLIN** I understand I'm gay. I want to lead a normal, healthy life. And I will.

**MAM** You're breaking my heart. You're breaking my bleeding heart.

**COLIN** Mam, you're not listening. You just don't want to hear. I'm gay. Gay gay gay gay gay!

**MAM** I'm off. This is disgusting. You shovelling your shit in my face.

**COLIN** You're my mam. What d'you expect?

**MAM** I expect you to marry a nice girl. Settle down and have some kids. Bring them down the Gower in the summer holidays. And we'll nurture those kids in a proper environment. See that they're healthy. That they grows up proper. Like we did with you and our Keith.

**COLIN** Only I turned out queer. What'll you do if these fine healthy grandchildren turn out queer? Eh Mam? What then?

**MAM** You're perverted Colin. You're twisting everything.

**COLIN** Because you won't see. You won't understand.

**MAM** I can't! I can't understand! Can't you see that? I don't understand it at all. Why Colin why?

*She starts to cry. He goes to her. She won't let him touch her. The doorbell rings.*

**MAM** Jesus that's your father. Not a word. Not a bleeding word. It'll break his bastard heart.

**COLIN** Alright. (*He goes to the circular window and shouts out*) Dad! Is that you?

**DAD** Hello Colin.

**COLIN** I'm dropping the key. (*He lowers the latchkey on a string out of the window).* There's someone with Dad. Who's that with Dad?

**MAM** That's the surprise. We got a surprise for you. All spoilt now. Everything's spoilt now.

**COLIN** Come on, Mam. Don't be such a drama queen.

**MAM** Where's the bathroom. I got to fix my face.

**COLIN** In there.

**MAM** Not a word. Not a bleeding word.

**COLIN** Mum's the word, Mam.

*She goes into the bathroom. A train rumbles past. COLIN closes the window and opens the doors to the stairs. We hear DAD's voice approaching.*

**DAD** Them trains rumble close by Col.

*DAD enters handing COLIN the latchkey.*

**DAD** Concierge service 'an all.

**COLIN** *(Smiling.)* Hello Dad.

*They shake hands, then hug. Standing in the door is ARI, clutching several Hamleys shopping bags.*

**COLIN** Good God!

*DAD laughs. ARI grins.*

**COLIN** It's Ari. It's bleeding Aristopolous. Good God. Come in. Come in.

*ARI and COLIN embrace.*

**ARI** Hello Colin. How are you?

**COLIN** It's Ari bleeding Stopolous and he's speaking English.

**ARI** I learn English. Now I speak well.

**COLIN** Bloody well. Bloody hell, I don't believe it.

**DAD** A surprise. We wanted to surprise you. Where's Mam?

**COLIN** In the bog.

**DAD** Oh. So this is it. Our boy's London pad.

**COLIN** That's it Dad. You look well.

**DAD** I am son. Bastard fit; I joined the squash.

**COLIN** And Ari looks great.

**ARI** Colin looks fantastic. He's changed. Not boy. Colin is man.

**DAD** His bastard English. Kills me. I took him to Hamleys.

**ARI** I buy presents for Greece. For my cousins. My nephews and nieces.

**DAD**　　Stocked up for all the family. He's an orphan. Eh Ari? No mam and dad.

**ARI**　　Brother, sister, nephew, niece, cousin.

**DAD**　　His bastard English.

**COLIN**　　Sit down, come on. What d'you want to drink?

**ARI**　　This is Colin's painting.

**COLIN**　　Yes.

**ARI**　　This is fantastic painting.

**COLIN**　　Thank you.

**ARI**　　These are books? Sketching books?

**COLIN**　　Yes.

**ARI**　　I can look?

**COLIN**　　Course. Course you can. Now what can I offer you?

*MAM enters.*

**MAM**　　No, we won't stop now. How was Hamleys? Look at Ari, Colin. Can you believe him? Isn't he great? He arrived last Wednesday. No we won't stop now. We'll get back to the hotel.

**DAD**　　But we're seeing you tonight? We're all having dinner tonight?

**COLIN**　　Yes Dad. Course we are.

**MAM**　　We'll be off then.

**DAD**　　Are you alright Mam?

**MAM**　　Got a bit of an headache that's all.

**DAD**　　Alright then. It's a great pad Colin.

**COLIN**  You don't say pad Dad. That's from another era. The trendy word is loft.

**DAD**  Loft off you cheeky sod.

**ARI**  Good. Book is fantastic, Colin. This one is fantastic.

*COLIN looks.*

**COLIN**  That's you Ari. In Kos. After that day, remember?

**ARI**  Yes I remember. Always. Always I think about it.

**MAM**  Come on Dad. Let's be off.

**DAD**  Aye alright.

**MAM**  Alright, Ari?

**ARI**  Yes.

**DAD**  We'll see you tonight son? Meet you at the restaurant.

**COLIN**  Course.

**ARI**  Bye Colin. (*They embrace.*) I see you again. Always I see you again.

**COLIN**  Course.

**MAM**  Come on, Ari. See you later, Colin.

*She takes ARI's arm and leaves without kissing COLIN. DAD and COLIN are left alone.*

**DAD**  Are you alright son?

**COLIN**  Yes Dad.

**DAD**  You told her didn't you?

**COLIN**  What Dad? Told her what?

**DAD** About you. Being... well, being gay isn't it?

**COLIN** Dad I don't believe you.

**DAD** Come here you soft bastard. (*He gives COLIN a bear hug.*) You big soft bastard. What bastard difference does it make? You're my frigging son and I'm proud of you. Any bastard at work makes fun of queers and I'll kick his fucking head in.

**MAM** Dad! Come on! Hurry up!

**DAD** Aye alright! Don't worry about Mam son. She'll come round. It doesn't make a jot of bastard difference I can tell you. You're my Brick Lane boyo – keeping ahead of the pack.

*He goes.*

**COLIN** Dad!

*He turns.*

**DAD** What?

**COLIN** Thanks.

**DAD** Get on you big soft bastard.

*He goes. The saxophone starts up and the lights fade to total darkness. The saxophone fades and COLIN is in bed, in his underpants. The outside light shines into the room through the circular windows. The doorbell rings. COLIN stirs. He sits up and checks his watch. The doorbell rings again. COLIN gets out of bed and goes to the window. He opens it and shouts down.*

**COLIN** Hello! Hello, who is it?

**JAMES** Colin? Is that you Colin? It's me, James.

**COLIN** James!

**JAMES**     Can I come in? Is that you Colin? Will you let me in?

**COLIN**     Yes hold on. I'll drop the key. (*throws the latchkey down on a string.*) Here. Can you see it?

**JAMES**     Thanks.

**COLIN**     Bloody hell, bloody James.

*He closes the window and opens the door to the stairway. He sits on his bed, propped against the pillows. JAMES enters.*

**JAMES**     Christ! Those stairs! Where are you? It's dark.

**COLIN**     It's night. It's the middle of the night.

**JAMES**     There you are. Nearly naked. God you look sexy. (*He goes to COLIN and touches his bare back.*) Let me kiss you.

**COLIN**     Don't be soft. You been drinking.

**JAMES**     I been out.

**COLIN**     It's late.

**JAMES**     So? Don't be anal. God you're beautiful.

**COLIN**     Leave off James. I've had enough for one day.

*He gets a sweatshirt and puts it on.*

**JAMES**     Why?

**COLIN**     My parents. They been up. I had dinner with them. Told them I was gay.

**JAMES**     Bloody hell. Who the fuck comes out to their parents! You like life heavy, don't you, Colin?

*JAMES switches on a bedside lamp.*

**COLIN**   D'you have to? I was asleep. Still am. Half-asleep.

**JAMES**   I want to see you properly.

**COLIN**   Why? I don't hear from you for ten days and then you show up in the middle of the night. Why? You're mad.

**JAMES**   God you're sexy. What did they say?

**COLIN**   Who?

**JAMES**   Your people?

**COLIN**   Not a lot. Well Mam sounded off. She's got the hump. But Dad was brilliant. Anyhow we couldn't talk about it tonight.

**JAMES**   Why?

**COLIN**   They was with a friend. Remember that Greek bloke. He was over.

**JAMES**   Ari? How horny! Did you make a pass?

**COLIN**   What's the matter with you?

**JAMES**   Nothing. He looked sexy that's all.

**COLIN**   What are you doing here James?

**JAMES**   Fine friend you are.

**COLIN**   Well I don't understand. And I'm tired. Today's been rough.

**JAMES**   Rough for who? Oh Colin!

*JAMES looks in complete despair. He throws his arms around COLIN. COLIN embraces him.*

**COLIN**   Jesus! Come on mush! What's the matter? I'm sorry. I didn't mean to be short. It's alright.

*JAMES breaks away. He sits down.*

**COLIN**  Oh Jesus! You did it! You did it, didn't you? You took the test? You took the bleeding test. The bleeding blood test. The bloody bleeding, bleeding bloody blood test. (*A pause. JAMES nods.*) And? And? You're positive. (*JAMES nods.*) Oh fuck! Fucking shit! James I'm sorry. I really am. I'm so sorry.

*He goes to JAMES.*

**JAMES**  Don't touch me!

**COLIN**  When? When did you find out?

**JAMES**  Five o'clock tonight. I tested this morning. You can get same day results now. I've known for eight hours.

**COLIN**  James. Oh Christ, James.

**JAMES**  So Mr. Wise-One, what do you say now?

**COLIN**  I just say it's better to know where you stand.

**JAMES**  That's easy for you to say. You're sitting pretty. Ever since last time. Since I saw you last. I've been obsessed. Obsessed with this fucking issue. I've been over and over it. Should I or shouldn't I? I've been for counselling. Weighed up all the pros and cons. You know I couldn't get a mortgage now? Couldn't get life insurance. Big deal, who wants all that crap? I'm almost certain to get full blown AIDS. Eventually. Then I'll die.

**COLIN**  That's not true. You can do things now. Safeguard now. Things to help you never get ill. Things to make sure you stay healthy.

**JAMES**  Yes and get a tonload of toxic shit pumped into my system at the same time.

**COLIN**  That's rubbish! There's lots of alternatives. You don't smoke. D'you do drugs?

**JAMES**  Not exactly.

**COLIN**  You should give up drink. Do a really ace diet.

**JAMES**  Don't preach to me. Don't fucking preach to me!

**COLIN**  James, listen to me! There's people out there with HIV. They've been exposed to this virus for years. Their immune systems are A1. Operating brilliantly. We can live with this virus. It's been proven. People can live with this virus in their systems.

**JAMES**  I'm not people.

**COLIN**  Bullshit! I wish for your sake you were negative. But you're not.

*COLIN holds JAMES.*

**JAMES**  I'm scared.

**COLIN**  Me too. Nearly all the time. But they say fear eats the soul. So we gotta push on.

*JAMES breaks away. The saxophone starts up.*

**JAMES**  Christ Colin where do you get off? You're like a fucking saint. Saint fucking Colin.

**COLIN**  Fuck off! D'you want to spend the night?

**JAMES**  Do I fucking ever? I want to cling to you as the last vestige of sanity on this spiralling fucking universe of turd. I want to hold onto your goodliness and smother myself in it until I breathe into new life, into something recognizably human. I want to crawl from the sewer and the stench and drink in your fountain of purity and wisdom and bathe in your sense and sensibility. I want to be baptised in your saliva and grow strong in your aura and climax in your brilliant light. And walk down the path of that light until I can see beyond the foulness and degradation and into the openness and hope of a new tomorrow. Of a new start. Of a brightness and optimism and a way to wash away all the filth, all the vermin and lice.

*A pause.*

**COLIN**   You're pissed.

**JAMES**   What if I am?

*JAMES goes and lies on the bed. COLIN turns off the bedside lamp. The telephone rings ... and rings, then stops.*

**JAMES**   The answer machine could have got that. (*COLIN moves towards the bed.*) Wrap yourself around me. Please! Breathe all over my face. (*COLIN lies down and embraces JAMES.*) I love you. (*A pause.*) There's only one word for you Colin. You're wise. That's it. Wise.

**COLIN**   Sssh!

**JAMES** (*Falling asleep.*) Wise.

*The saxophone rises up like a siren as the lights fade to black.*

# ACT THREE

*The roof-top of a house in the medina at Essaouira in Morocco. White walls of varying shapes overlook the beach and sea. In the roof there is an enormous skylight which looks down to the ground floor of the house. Several doors off. Various mullahs chant the call to prayer. Every fifteen minutes the nearby clock tower rings out its bells.*

*COLIN is sitting in a rattan chair. There is an ignored but open book resting on his lap. He wears sunshades and is older. He stares into the distance. AICHA, a fine-looking Moroccan woman in her forties is taking a white sheet off a clothes line. She is dressed in white overalls and a white turban. She detaches the line at one end and hooks it to the wall. She folds the sheet and brushes past COLIN. He stirs. She smiles at him, then leaves. The call to prayer ceases.*

**COLIN** Wise. That's hilarious. Bloody wise. Bleeding wise. Bleeding bloody well bleeding wise. (*He takes off his glasses.*) Well wisdom has brought me a long way. Brought me South. South to Essaouira. There's only the desert after this and then I'll be free...When I woke up the next morning, James had gone. Left a note, "Sorry, you were right. I was pissed." The warning bells should have flared then, but I'm daft. (*He rolls a joint. A kestrel in a cage starts to flap its wings. COLIN turns to the bird.*) Calm down. Calm down poor thing. You can't get out. You're symbolic. A symbol. It's one of the few bonuses round 'ere, the kif. Helps you to let go. Not cling to the wreckage. Of your past. She'll be here in a minute. We're expecting her any minute now. We're in need of a good laugh. Just got to tip her the wink and she's on a plane. That's what it's like for a career girl with no domestic ties. I've been in Essaouira now for ten months and I still can't believe how I've managed to stay out of trouble. Course Ari's been a great help. Looks out for me. He's always stood by me, ever since that first summer. Much to Mam's chagrin. I come up here to read. Up on the roof. But all I seem to do is day-dream. Some habits linger a lifetime.

*COLIN picks up his book and starts to read. SHELLEY appears in the doorway to the stairs. She is clearly older, tougher looking but still with a lot of energy. She watches COLIN for a few moments. He doesn't notice her.*

**SHELLEY** As usual. On your tod.

**COLIN** Shelley!

**SHELLEY** Hiya.

*COLIN goes to her.*

**COLIN** Oh Shelley.

*He starts to tremble. She holds him. ARI has appeared in the doorway to the stairs.*

**SHELLEY** There. That's alright. I'm here now. I'll take care.

**COLIN** I've almost given up.

**SHELLEY** Don't talk soft.

*COLIN breaks away. He wipes his eyes.*

**COLIN** Jesus Ari, don't snoop about!

**ARI** Not snoop Colin. I bring Shelley. La Bomb-shell. I go to bus station. Here she is.

**SHELLEY** Bomb-shell! You cheeky so and so.

**ARI** You are. Bomb-shell Shelley.

**COLIN** Ask Aicha to organize some tea, eh?

**ARI** Aicha she prepare now. I go. Bring tea. I see you later Shelley.

**SHELLEY** Aye, thanks love. Thanks for the ride. (*ARI goes.*) Christ Col, there's a looker.

**COLIN** I wouldn't advise making a bee-line.

**SHELLEY** Why not?

**COLIN** It's a long story.

**SHELLEY** Christ Col, that journey from Marrakech. There's a riot. People were moving house I reckon. I've never seen so much junk piled on the roof of one bus. One woman had a bleeding turkey. And they shoved that on the roof an' all. Feet tied. Poor bastard. He'll be happier stuffed. I'm telling you, it's a funny country this, Col.

**COLIN** It's a wonder there wasn't a goat on the roof-rack.

**SHELLEY** Give over.

*AICHA brings in a tray with Moroccan mint tea.*

**COLIN** Ah Aicha, ça c'est Shelley. Une amie du Pays de Galles.

**AICHA** Bonjour, ça va? C'est vrai, Portugal? C'est un pays bon, oui?

**COLIN** Pas Portugal. Pays de Galles. W.A.L.E.S.

**AICHA** Ah! Oui! Vous voulez du thé?

**SHELLEY** I stop at diolchn yn fawr, love.

**COLIN** Elle parle pas Francais.

**AICHA** Moi, pas d'Anglais.

*She laughs aloud. COLIN grins.*

**COLIN** Don't look so shell-shocked.

**SHELLEY** Get on. Haven't heard that for yonks.

**COLIN** Aicha is the mother of the household. C'est vrai Maman? Vous-etes Maman.

**AICHA** Oui. Il est mon fils. Thé à la menthe.

**COLIN** Shokran Aicha.

**AICHA** La shokran elle wajib.

*She goes.*

**SHELLEY** Blimey, slaves. There's crachach.

**COLIN** We speak to one another in terrible French. That way we can conduct some sort of relationship.

**SHELLEY** God help!

*COLIN lights the joint. He hands it to SHELLEY.*

**COLIN** I'm glad you're here, Shell. Hak.

**SHELLEY** Come again.

**COLIN** It means take.

**SHELLEY** Blimey! You're the spit of a living Arab.

**COLIN** When in Essaouira.

**SHELLEY** I bet you're stoned all the time. No thanks, love. If I even smell the stuff I make Noddy seem real.

**COLIN** Ashtra?

**SHELLEY** Give over.

**COLIN** It means "what's up?"

**SHELLEY** Not you that's for sure.

**COLIN** Think I've changed?

**SHELLEY** You looks tired love.

**COLIN** I am. How's my mother, then?

**SHELLEY** I've heard she's fit. Keith's still living with her, mind! I think the divorce upset him. Her going off with another fella and then refusing to either marry or live tally with him.

**COLIN** About six months after I told her I was gay I went down to Swansea and she picked me up at the station. I got in the car and she said "I'm sorry Colin but I'd sooner you were dead". (*A pause.*) I worry about Dad. He took the divorce badly. Writes all the time. I dunno what to say. Keeps asking questions about my being gay. (*SHELLEY mock gasps.*) Good of you to come, Shell.

**SHELLEY** Your letter was so desperate.

**COLIN** Was it?

**SHELLEY** Come on.

**COLIN** Oh you know how moods take you. Everything changes.

**SHELLEY** All got too much for you, eh?

**COLIN** Probably. It is all too much for me. Feel like I'm dying. Anyway I can't talk about it. Not yet.

*A pause.*

**SHELLEY** Are you painting?

**COLIN** That's a joke. Can't think when I last painted. Painter's block. I did when I first came here. But I've been too tired. There's been too much to do. Looking after him.

**SHELLEY** You've got the kif and the Moroccans. You've got the fisherman... Abder?

**COLIN** Abderahim.

**SHELLEY** Aberafon, That's him.

**COLIN** Aberafon! Fuck Off! Stupid thing is I'm so in love even the idea of leaving the house – well it's a joke. I would have to sit in cafés and wait for him to finish playing pool. Reduced to a teenage moll. And 'cos I can't bring him here, for one reason or another, it's down to the occasional blow-job on the beach.

**SHELLEY** Sounds familiar.

**COLIN** The worst thing is he doesn't need me to be in love with him. He'll probably go ape when he sees you. Tits are more his territory. (*There is a loud coughing from behind one of the doorways.*) He's awake. The very mention of Aberafon makes him go all chesty.

**SHELLEY** You should be flattered.

**COLIN** Go and say hello. And Shell. Don't look too shell-shocked.

*She goes to the room where the coughing has now subsided. She pokes her head around the door, screams loudly and retreats.*

**SHELLEY** Christ, Col, what is it?

**COLIN** That's AIDS, love. That's what it does.

**SHELLEY** I don't mean James. I didn't even see him. There's all these ... things. These things everywhere. Bloody creatures.

**COLIN**  Oh, that. They're the chameleons.

**SHELLEY** There's bleeding hundreds.

**COLIN**  A slight exaggeration. They're supposed to blend.

*JAMES enters. He is greatly changed. He looks about fifty and is very thin. His hair loss is noticeable and his face is a mass of purple blotches.*

**JAMES**  It's envy which draws me to them Shelley. I am the one who wishes to blend. But you, being the canny South Walean saw right through the chameleons. Presumably you'll know me for the phoney that I really am. Well come on. Give me a hug and get it over with. I know I make the Elephant Man seem cute but there it is.

**COLIN**  If we're gonna be treated to the constant stream of scintillating self-deprecation, I'm off out.

**JAMES**  In search of Moroccan cock? Or do I mean Abderahim? I never quite know the difference.

**COLIN**  James?

**JAMES**  Colin?

**COLIN**  Get lost. Give you two time to bond.

*As COLIN goes.*

**JAMES**  Any more lost my dear and you shan't know me from a chameleon. Whoosh. And off he goes. Come on Shelley, give us a hug. (*SHELLEY hugs him.*) There. That's better. I feel loved again.

**SHELLEY** Love hurts.

**JAMES** Tell me about it.

**SHELLEY** I brought some Stoly. Duty Free.

**JAMES** Let's do it.

**SHELLEY** It's in my room. I'll get it.

*SHELLEY goes. James start to cough severely.*

**JAMES** Jesus, that fucking cloud looks like a snowstorm erupting. Fucking white thing! Uh? What d 'you say Kestrel? Don't be stupid. They can't let you out. If they let you out there'll be no-one lower than me.

*SHELLEY enters.*

**SHELLEY** Here, this'll bring colour to your cheeks.

**JAMES** If we could find my cheeks amongst the KS, I'm sure they'd celebrate.

*She pours the vodka.*

**JAMES** You hungry?

**SHELLEY** Not at all. Stuffed myself in Marrakech.

**JAMES** What are you doing here?

**SHELLEY** Colin.

**JAMES** Asked you to come?

**SHELLEY** Not really. I've come for Colin.

**JAMES** Not me?

**SHELLEY** Well ...

**JAMES** Good. 'Cos I don't need you. I'll be dead soon, and I shan't need anything more.

**SHELLEY** James, don't say that.

**JAMES** Come on Shelley wise up. You're a smart lass. You know the score.

**SHELLEY** I've never understood you James. I know I hardly knows you. But from everything Colin's told me.

**JAMES** That'll be a fairly unfairly biased viewpoint.

**SHELLEY** Come on, ease up.

**JAMES** Oh fuck off. No. No. It's nothing. It's me. Just me. AIDS-ridden me. At least I'm not in denial.

**SHELLEY** Rage more like.

**JAMES** If only. Deep-rooted cynicism. I've spent my entire life running away.

**SHELLEY** From Colin.

**JAMES** Amongst others. But Colin is such a major ... fucking "arsehole", I've always run back. He's the only one.

**SHELLEY** I don't know why he puts up with you.

**JAMES** Colin is the only nice person God ever created. But even Colin's looking beat up these days. His goodliness has overstepped the parameter into masochism. He's in love with the unobtainable. But then ... he always has been.

**SHELLEY** Why did you come here? To Essaouira.

**JAMES** Why? I wanted to take my sorrow elsewhere. My shame. My sores. Colin's life in London had become uncreative. Hanging out in nightclubs. I was getting sicker and he became adrift.

**SHELLEY** And here?

**JAMES** This vodka's good. I'm not supposed to drink. But I've said fuck it. I'm living in one of the most beautiful places on earth, I'm going to have a little fun. And what about you, Shelley? How's your love life?

**SHELLEY** Oh, a nightmare! I think I'll go lesbian. Find some nice girl who'll love me for the fat cow I am and settle down in cosy bliss. Blueberry soup and turtle pie.

**JAMES** Wow.

**SHELLEY** No, it's not all bad. I'm Chief Supervisor at a market research group in the West End. Decent money, a position of responsibility, quite a good giggle, and bloody hard work. Leaving little time for any play – I'm alone in the world see, totally alone. There was only me and Mam. Now there's only me.

**JAMES** Can't wait for Colin to come back. The three of us can have a party.

**SHELLEY** You asked. I'm not being maudlin. Them's the facts.

**JAMES** I know. I'm a cunt. Sorry, arsehole.

*ARI enters.*

**ARI** Ah Shelley. Hungry, huh? Aicha she prepare.

**JAMES** That's alright Ari, she got stuffed in Marrakech.

**SHELLEY** Give over. I'll stuff you in minute mush.

**ARI** Is good here, no?

**SHELLEY** Excellent. Not without its tensions of course.

**JAMES** Every home must have them. Besides, our troubles are nothing to Ari's.

**ARI** Troubles? What troubles I have? I leave Greece. I live London. Now I live Morocco. Is good life.

Colin is my friend. Like brother. And you. You are only trouble.

**JAMES**  Hear that? Bullied by my only remaining friend.

**ARI**  I jest. You are brother-in-law. (*ARI pours himself a vodka.*) I can?

**SHELLEY** Course.

**JAMES**  And how about your future mother-in-law, eh Ari?

**ARI**  Ah! Aicha's mother!

**SHELLEY** You getting married?

**JAMES**  He's going Moslem. (*They laugh.*) What's your name Ari? Your Moslem name?

**ARI**  Larbee.

**JAMES**  Larbee. The Arab.

**SHELLEY** Sorry boys. You've left me shipwrecked.

**JAMES**  Well Ari and Aicha made a little one. And now he has to marry Aicha. Or they'll shove her in some jail and confiscate the brat.

**SHELLEY** Never? Never! Ari!

*She laughs. The men join in.*

**ARI**  Aicha she go to police. To tell about petite. Now I must make Moslem.

**JAMES**  Become.

**ARI**  Yes.

**JAMES**  He's coming today, no? The man with the papers.

**ARI** He come now. Aicha she wait for him.

**JAMES** It's quite a place this Shell. A man can have many wives, but an unmarried mother, it's not on is it? Aicha has to carry a paper if she leaves this house at night to prove she's a maid and not a prostitute.

**SHELLEY** And another paper by day to prove she's a wife and not a concubine.

**JAMES** Very good.

**ARI** Is good? What is concubine? Concubine is good?

**SHELLEY** All them papers Ari, you'll have to buy her a briefcase.

*AICHA enters and picks up the tea-tray.*

**AICHA** Il est venu. L'homme avec les papiers.

**JAMES** Your time has come Larbee.

**AICHA** Ah Larbee. C'est lui.

**ARI** I come Aicha. Make Moslem for you.

**AICHA** Larbee. Ça c'est Larbee. C'est bien appellé.

*She goes laughing. JAMES laughs. ARI goes, turns back to JAMES and mock shoots him.*

**JAMES** A mélange of words.

**SHELLEY** Oh God I can't believe it.

**JAMES** What?

**SHELLEY** I fancies him rotten. To tell the truth gutless. I was looking forward to a good old-fashioned Mediterranean poke.

**JAMES** That sounds more like the old shell-shocked.

Anyway, nothing stopping you. A Moslem can have many wives.

**SHELLEY** Get on!

**JAMES** Wish I could recall the sensation of a Mediterranean poke. Occidental, Oriental, any poke memories would do.

**SHELLEY** Sorry, I didn't mean to be selfish.

**JAMES** There's still the odd hand-job, when the occasion arises. Rarely I'm afraid.

**SHELLEY** And Colin?

**JAMES** When he isn't pining, there is the odd cuddle. It seems Colin has to love someone he can't have or he isn't complete.

**SHELLEY** Look I'm not here to pry. I came to help out. Colin's my oldest mate.

**JAMES** I know. Isn't it amazing to think we're still young?

**SHELLEY** We've had to grow up fast us lot.

**JAMES** I look twice my age.

**SHELLEY** That's not true. (*JAMES coughs and splutters. He blows his nose.*) Are you getting the right attention? I mean here, in Africa?

**JAMES** Good God Shelley, look around, look at this house. Look at Aicha and Ari, sorry Larbee. Look at you. Look at the chameleons. They're my friends. They can change. Wish I could. Wish I could make this KS change colour. Hide. Disappear.

**SHELLEY** I don't mean that mush. I mean medicine. That might make the Kaposi disappear.

**JAMES** It's a matter of time.

**SHELLEY** And quality.

**JAMES** Exactly. The quality of my life here is greater. There's privacy. And warmth. And my people. My family.

**SHELLEY** And your other family? The Derwen Fawr lot?

**JAMES** They write the cheques. Look Shelley I didn't want to remain in England to have a bunch of crap ploughed through me so that I could stay awake for ten more diminishing minutes.

**SHELLEY** Fair enough. I'll leave it.

**JAMES** Dinner's at nine. A complete feast.

**SHELLEY** James?

**JAMES** Shelley?

**SHELLEY** D'you ever go out?

**JAMES** If I do, sometimes, it's in a hooded jellaba. I adopt the look of the Berber. I go and gaze at the Isle of Mogador. Why?

**SHELLEY** Just wondered. Where?

**JAMES** It's an island just off the coast. Used to house a prison. Then became a Lazaretto.

**SHELLEY** You what?

**JAMES** Get Colin to take you. Makes a lovely day trip. No-one's there but the gulls and the rabbits.

**SHELLEY** Sounds frisky.

**JAMES** Shelley?

**SHELLEY** Boyo?

**JAMES**   Let's have another cuddle.

**SHELLEY** Come 'ere you big soft bastard. Let's get hold of you. You're skin and bones boy.

*They hug. She goes.*

**JAMES**   That's better, I feel loved again. What d'you say Kezzy? Kezzy kestrel.

*JAMES looks weak and frail, in need of a rest. Quietly he starts to sing "Karma Chameleon". He slowly walks into his room singing to himself and the chameleons. The clock strikes six and the light fades. A Moroccan folk song, with drums and guitar is heard. It is a song for freedom.*

*COLIN is sitting alone on the terrace. It is night. The sounds fade.*

**COLIN**   You see James has a fantasy life. A secret life. A spiritual life. Whilst I've been so concerned with living things; with living things properly, I've become submerged. Submerged in reality. James listens to the chameleons or the kestrel, or Aicha, or the chanting mullahs, or the clocks, the sea, the occasional rain, the cats, the endless shuffling of medina feet, whistling boys, ruffian children, home-going workmen. It's an endless game of how many amusements you can think up, but then, you have to find them amusing or you get bored. I'm not even excited about cassettes from London. I am unable to separate myself from him. Siametically tied. And here he is, closer to death than any of us, and here he is, our teacher. Confusion reigns. But it's nice up here at night. And he sleeps there, over by there. It's his blood, his bloody blood. It's all inside his bleeding red bloody bleeding blood. Neither Aicha nor Ari is the greatest conversationalist of the twentieth century. So I'm up on the roof a lot. Thing is

I can't really work out what medicine he's taking, 'cos he's determined to keep control. And I always think you should respond to a strong person in the way they expect you to respond; and hope you've read their mind properly. That bloody blood.

*SHELLEY enters out of breath.*

**SHELLEY** Christ Col, them stairs, I can hardly puff up 'em. Steep mind, ain't they? Aicha and Ari were in the kitchen talking a rare language that I don't think either of them could understand. So I thought I'd best leave before there's a middle-eastern crisis. Bit of the old macho isn't he? You're on your tod as usual. I was thinking about James you know, love him, and I was just wondering if he'd like a blow-job. Well, I s'pose that's a bit risky, but a hand-job at least. Course not from me necessarily, but we could air-lift one in. What d'you reckon?

**COLIN** About what?

**SHELLEY** A hand-job.

**COLIN** No thanks Shell.

**SHELLEY** Not you, you pillock. Him over there. Your Jimbo. He don't look well Col.

**COLIN** That's 'cos he's dying.

**SHELLEY** Shurrup! He's only by there.

**COLIN** It's something he likes talking about. Something he encourages. It's very wearying, but ... (*he pauses*) essential. He looks that way because the poor bugger's been attacked on every front. But his eyes are like jewels. Anthracite jewels. Dark and vibrant. And his tongue is like the snake he really is. We can really see the serpent now. Pure reptile family.

**SHELLEY** I was never very cosy with Derwen Fawr. It's funny mind isn't it? 'Cos I don't know him very well. But I'm getting to know him now. It's been less than a week, but I've settled down. And I hope I've helped him a bit. I've done a few like, personal things. But mostly he's very private that way.

**COLIN** It's support. For the whole household.

**SHELLEY** And I'm pert.

**COLIN** Fuck off. Where's that fucking vodka? I'd love a drink.

**SHELLEY** It's drunk love.

**COLIN** A joint?

**SHELLEY** You're pretty stoned already. I reckon a good kip.

**COLIN** I can't unwind. It's like I'm tumbling off the edge of the earth. Caught in a ravine of ideas and unable to move a muscle.

**SHELLEY** I'm desperate to get into Ari's knickers. Christ he's gorgeous even if he is a macho pig. Sometimes I'm terrified to eat the soup in case Aicha's dropped in a dead chameleon or some finger nails.

**COLIN** Don't worry, it's not you she'll poison. It's him. Larbee.

**SHELLEY** D'you reckon?

**COLIN** I know. Macho he may be, but he won't get the better of Aicha. Everything's topsy-turvy here in Essaouira.

**SHELLEY** Makes a change from North-West Six.

**COLIN** So you reckon Aicha smells tart?

**SHELLEY** Less of your lip young man. Unless it's on my vagina.

**COLIN** Shelley, you are filthy.

**SHELLEY** Yeah, you always say that. I can always shut you up. Mr Goody Two-Shoes. See I was so dead impressed with the whole corruption of your being gay that I never noticed you was a right no-hoper.

**COLIN** What d'you mean?

**SHELLEY** Well I had to come to terms with the fact that you were a sexual no-hoper. But I never applied it to life.

**COLIN** What d 'you mean?

**SHELLEY** You've saddled yourself here love.

**COLIN** You mean this one-horse town?

**SHELLEY** In which you appear to be the horse.

**COLIN** What?

**SHELLEY** Well you're always popping out. What d'you get up to out there?

**COLIN** Shell you don't think? You don't imagine I'm the fag of Essaouira. Endless head on the beach and a flash-in-the-pan poke up a dark alley. Hanging round the port to catch fisherman. It's too busy love. Too many people out there. You're never alone for ten seconds.

**SHELLEY** With my tits, you're never alone anyhow. Look it's nice to be here.

**COLIN** It isn't a barrel.

**SHELLEY** What's a coupla weeks? Besides we got to look after each other. If we don't look after each other, who's going to look after each other?

**COLIN**   That sounds deep Shell.

**SHELLEY** Yeah. I think I been inhaling some of your reefers.

**COLIN**   I think you're a soft cow.

**SHELLEY** And you're a no-hoper.

**COLIN**   James is the one. He's the chameleon. Calm and constantly changing.

**SHELLEY** And when he's gone?

**COLIN**   Don't. Don't think about it.

**SHELLEY** That's what this is all about, eh? The ones who are left behind. It's about us. About you.

**COLIN**   There's always the desert. I'll be alright.

**SHELLEY** Sure you will. Hopefully you'll paint again. Find some job. Move on. But look at you now.

**COLIN**   I'm worn out that's all. I once told James that fear eats the soul, that's because I could push on, see clearly, but now my soul is ravaged.

**SHELLEY** Colin, I wish I could help you.

**COLIN**   Save me.

**SHELLEY** From what?

**COLIN**   There's awakening, realisation, then consequence. This is the consequence.

**SHELLEY** Of what? Being gay?

**COLIN**   No. Being alive

**SHELLEY** But you're young love. Look Col, I watched Mam die, and a mate of mine in London. From AIDS. And it's the end. The end of many things. It becomes the end of many things for many people. But it's not the end of everything.

**COLIN** I just wish he'd die tonight. Then I could let go. Hearing him coughing, waiting for a new KS to appear. Freaking about his lungs every time his temperature rises, looking and watching, worrying about his sleep. But he's strong. He's strong and fighting.

**SHELLEY** They say people go when they want to go.

**COLIN** Give us a cuddle Shell.

*They hug.*

**SHELLEY** I'm always on call for a cuddle.

**COLIN** It's 'cos you're substantial. D'you mind?

**SHELLEY** Hates it. Hate physical contact. Yeugh! I'm going to slip a mogadon in Aicha's tea. Then seduce her Moslem husband.

**COLIN** I love you Shell.

**SHELLEY** I love you too mush.

**COLIN** If we don't look after each other, who's going to look after each other?

**SHELLEY** You said it.

**COLIN** I think you did, actually, Shell.

**SHELLEY** Aye Right. I'm off for a bit of shut-eye. You alright?

**COLIN** Hunky-Dory.

**SHELLEY** Andy Warhol looks a scream. Hang him on my wall.

*COLIN laughs.*

**COLIN** Andy Warhol silver screen.

**SHELLEY** Can't tell him apart at all.

*She kisses COLIN. She goes.*

**COLIN** Ciao Bella. Can't tell him apart at all. (*He walks to JAMES' room, stands in the doorway.*) Can't tell him apart at all. (*He disappears into JAMES' room.*)

*SHELLEY quietly enters, goes to the bird-cage and takes out the kestrel. She takes him to the wall overlooking the sea and lets him go.*

**SHELLEY** There!

*She leaves. The lights fade. The sound of screeching gulls. Later the same night. Not a sound save the softly crashing sea. The moon is full. COLIN sits alone.*

**COLIN** I heard the clock strike two and I come out 'ere. I think I was dropping off. To tell the truth I'm contemplating another joint. James says I'm like a lazy Moroccan. Too much sun and too much smoke. Maybe I'll wander down the port. It's calm tonight. Good fishing.

*ARI and DAD enter.*

**ARI** Is here. Is roof. Ah! Here is Colin. Look who is.

**COLIN** Hang on a sec. You can't be serious. Dad? Dad is that you?

**DAD** Well it's not the king of Morocco.

**COLIN** Jesus!

**DAD** Nor him.

**ARI** He come now. Take taxi from Marrakech. Nice Mercedes Benz. Nice icey-blue. He knocking, then me, I wake up.

**COLIN**     I didn't hear a thing. Hello Dad.

*He shakes his father's hand. A pause. They embrace, then laugh.*

**DAD**     Look at Ari. Can't believe him. Head of the house.

**ARI**     Chief cook, bottle wash. I have baby. Pretty Moroc baby. Little girl. La Petite.

**DAD**     Good God son, you're a swift worker. Where's the missus?

**ARI**     Is where?

**DAD**     Your wife.

**ARI**     Not already. Making the marriage soon. Beautiful Moroc woman. She in kitchen. Make tea.

**DAD**     You wanna watch yourself over 'ere son. They'll chop off your hands. Let alone your odds and sods.

**COLIN**     Well Dad, what d'you fancy? You must be dead beat. You hungry?

**DAD**     No son. Not at all. Drop o' tea wouldn't go amiss. And I brought some whiskey. Off the plane. That'd go down well.

**ARI**     Aicha she come. Bring tea. Me, I fetch whiskey.

**DAD**     It's in the yellow carrier, Ari.

**ARI**     Duty Free. Me, I know it.

*He goes. A pause.*

**COLIN**     Is everything alright?

**DAD** Look Col. I'm sorry son. Sorry to shock you. Like this. All unannounced, and in the middle of the night. But there's things.

**COLIN** What things?

**DAD** Things. Things I can't explain. Not yet. Things.

**COLIN** What things?

**DAD** You don't remember do you?

**COLIN** What, Dad?

**DAD** That's what you said to me and your mother when you left home. When you first left Swansea. You said there were things.

**COLIN** What things?

**DAD** That's what I've come to find out. What things?

*SHELLEY enters.*

**SHELLEY** Christ I can't swallow it. I can't give it bleeding credence.

**DAD** Hello Shell.

**SHELLEY** It's really true? Well hiya. How's it going?

*They hug.*

**DAD** Not bad love. Not bad at all. I've come to have a chat with Colin.

**SHELLEY** It's a long way for a conversation. Lines to Morocco down, were they?

**DAD** Well...

**SHELLEY** Anyway lovely to see you, but I'm not about to

interrupt. Just wanted to say hiya, and to tell you Colin that Aicha's a bit heavy-like. Sleepy-heavy.

**COLIN** Uh?

**SHELLEY** You know. Aicha. She took a pill.

**COLIN** What?

**SHELLEY** One of mine.

**COLIN** Aicha had one of your mogadon?

**SHELLEY** Yeah. Yeah.

**COLIN** Shelley! You never?

**SHELLEY** Yeah. She was a bit over-tired. Funny enough I was entertaining Ari when your dad arrived.

**COLIN** You're a cheeky slut.

**SHELLEY** Don't mind him.

**DAD** No, go on you.

**SHELLEY** I don't think Ari should have disturbed her. But he would insist. Got her out of bed. Turban an' all. Too much chauvinism in this world, eh Mr Rhys?

**DAD** Call me Harry, love. After all, it's you kids who seem like the grown-ups here, and me the lost child.

**COLIN** I don't believe you, Dad. What the fuck are you doing here?

**DAD** My own flesh. Welcome like that.

**SHELLEY** Oh love him. He's had a big journey Col.

**DAD** No Colin is right. I am behaving erratically. But all the time these days. That's my lot.

*ARI enters followed by AICHA, drowsily carrying a tea tray.*

**ARI** I bring whiskey, looks good. You want something to eat? Something special? Sandwich. With Kefta. Or some fish?

**DAD** No thanks mate. Cup o' tea to steady me, then a drop o' whiskey to swill things round.

*AICHA puts down the tea tray. SHELLEY hovers over her.*

**AICHA** Bonjour. Tout le monde a bien dormi? Vous-voulez un oeuf? Du café? Voilà le thé. Pourquoi le thé?

**SHELLEY** See Col. See what I means.

**COLIN** Thank you, Shelley.

**SHELLEY** It's the night love. Middle of the bleeding night.

**AICHA** Comment?

**COLIN** Ce n'est pas le matin, Aicha. C'est tard. C'est la nuit. Mon père est ici.

**AICHA** C'est la nuit. (*She looks up at the sky.*) C'est la nuit. Mais qu'est-ce qu'il y a?

**COLIN** Mon père. Il est venu.

**AICHA** Oui. Bonjour. Je suis fatiguée. Mal à la tête. Le chat est là?

**SHELLEY** Come on cherub. You needs a bit o' shut-eye. I'll guide you down them steps.

**COLIN** Very magnanimous, Shell. Why d'you wake her up Ari?

**ARI** She make tea.

**COLIN** Well you could have done that.

**ARI** Me? Make tea?

**COLIN** Yes. I don't see why not. You don't wake someone up who's fast asleep, just to make a pot of bloody tea.

**SHELLEY** Come on girl. Time for bed.

*AICHA and SHELLEY go.*

**COLIN** She's doped out of her brain.

**ARI** Hashish. She smoke too much.

**COLIN** No she didn't. Don't be so bloody wise.

**DAD** Alright Col. Leave it now. Let's have a whiskey.

**ARI** He is angry. Now always angry.

**COLIN** Oh fuck off Ari. You know what's going on. Just fuck off.

**DAD** Hey Col. Leave it.

**ARI** I take whiskey. I go.

*He pours a whiskey then leaves.*

**COLIN** Ari! *(ARI stops.)* It doesn't matter. It doesn't matter. Nothing does.

**ARI** No Colin. It matters. Everything it matters. Painting. No painting. It matters. James. Matters. Shelley make us laugh. Matters. Your father come here. It matters. No Colin. Matters. Everything it matters.

*He goes.*

**COLIN** I used to think that an' all. Now ... I dunno.

**DAD** What's the matter Col? You look done in.

**COLIN** I am Dad. This isn't a holiday camp you know.

**DAD** I know that son. I haven't come for no holiday.

**COLIN** More like an hospice. James is ill.

**DAD** I know that son. How is he?

**COLIN** I mean very ill. I mean he's dying.

**DAD** Don't say that Col. Don't talk like that.

**COLIN** He's got AIDS Dad. AIDS. Understand?

**DAD** Look Colin, I'm not stupid. I read just now that AIDS is no longer an incurable disease. It's a serious but treatable condition.

**COLIN** If you wanna go through all that.

**DAD** All what?

**COLIN** Cocktails of drugs with side effects they can't always monitor. One ailment piling on top of another until it does your head in.

**DAD** Life is life, Colin.

**COLIN** Don't talk daft. Life is dying Dad. We're all of us slowly dying.

**DAD** I'm sorry Col. I feel sorry for you. Our Colin. Ever the optimist.

**COLIN** I wish he'd bloody well die tonight and we could all get on.

**DAD** Hey hush up. I was in a shop the other day and I saw a card, "Life's a bitch, and then you marry one." I got it in the kitchen. Where is James?

**COLIN** Over by there. Asleep. Is that how you feel? About Mam?

**DAD** No. Not really. A bit defensive still. No. It's more a state of confusion. You gets married, has kids, settle down, do well, make good money, a lovely house, and then, geronimo, you're falling off the world. Your son's gay and you love him, but it's something hard to understand. Your missus goes off with another bloke. And you love her. That's hard to understand. Your son's boyfriend's dying of AIDS. Maybe that's the hardest of all. I go home, eat cornflakes and get drunk. My life's in smithereens Col. And I don't know what to do.

**COLIN**  So you've come here. To find out.

**DAD**  Come to see you Col. To see how you're doing. What things? Eh? Things?

**COLIN**  Dad you're asking me to explain my whole life in one go. So it might enlighten yours. I love you. I love Mam, I s'pose. And our Keith. But I'm me. I'm Colin. We're all different.

**DAD**  I knows that Col. I'm not soft. But this gay business. When did you know? When did you cop on?

**COLIN**  Years ago.

**DAD**  Long before you told us?

**COLIN**  A while yes. Soon as I started getting horny. I s'pose I thought about boys. Cocks instead of tits. Is that what you want to hear?

**DAD**  I don't want to hear nothing Col. 'cept the truth. 'cept the truth.

**COLIN**  Why Dad, why? What's the use?

**DAD**  'Cos I've turned fifty, Col. And my life's in a whirlpool. I got to get it stopped. Then get it mobile again. D'you think lots of people are gay Col?

**COLIN**  Dunno. Quite a few.

**DAD**  But people hiding.

**COLIN**  You mean closets? Married people?

**DAD**   That sort of thing.

**COLIN**   Well, some of course. Lying through their teeth.

**DAD**   But how d'you know?

**COLIN**   What?

**DAD**   That you're gay.

**COLIN**   Dad! I dunno. Leave it. I told you. You fancies men. Men are in your fantasy life. You just want to be close to men.

**DAD**   But lots of married men are like that. I'm like that.

**COLIN**   Don't be soft. I don't mean that.

**DAD**   No I'm serious. At the club, where we plays squash. There's a sort of closeness. And after, in the showers, like a physical closeness. Not contact. Just a feeling like.

**COLIN**   Dad!

**DAD**   No I means it. And Ari. I always liked Ari. And when he slapped me on the back or pulled at my arm or gave me a wink, well, it warmed me up. That sort of thing.

**COLIN**   I dunno Dad. I'm not sure what you're saying. I think those are just normal things. Good things. They don't mean you're gay. It's not like you gave Ari a blow-job or nothing.

**DAD**   'Course not. Don't talk daft. But maybe I should have. Or got one from him at least.

**COLIN**   Dad! You're drunk.

**DAD**   Yeah. Reckon I am a bit. I dunno Colin.

I was faithful to your Mam. 'Course a few flirtations. But I never strayed. Now she's gone. I'm on my tod. And I dunno. I look at you. At your friends. And I wonder. Makes me stop to wonder. You're not near thirty and you're nursing a dying man. It wasn't like that when I was your age.

**COLIN**  I'm sorry Dad. Wish I could say something to make you understand. Make you feel better.

**DAD**  You can.

**COLIN**  What's that?

**DAD**  You can tell me I can stop over.

**COLIN**  Dad! 'Course you can.

**DAD**  I'll help out. Help with James. I've never met him you know. Never met anyone with AIDS. But I've watched Princess Di. She's great with them. On the telly.

**COLIN**  Yes Dad.

**DAD**  I want to learn. From you lot. To be with you. To change things for myself.

**COLIN**  Welcome to the madhouse.

**DAD**  Get on. (*A pause.*) It's late. Where d'you sleep Col?

**COLIN**  Up here. Close to James and the chameleons.

**DAD**  The chameleons?

**COLIN**  You'll meet them tomorrow. It's late. Even for me it's late.

**DAD**  Aye alright. Time for a kip. Thanks Col. Thanks.

**COLIN**  I'm glad you're here Dad.

**DAD** Yeah. (*They hug.*) Ari showed me my room. It's a grand house Colin. A fine place to live or die.

**COLIN** Get on. And you watch out for Ari in the night. He's a randy sod.

**DAD** Fuck off!

*He goes. COLIN looks bewildered, throws his eyes up to the skies.*

**COLIN** Paaalease!

*JAMES has appeared quietly in the doorway. He watches COLIN. He starts to cough. COLIN turns around. JAMES stops coughing.*

**JAMES** So that's my father-in-law?

**COLIN** Christ James. Don't startle me. I thought you were asleep.

**JAMES** You know me. Ever the chameleon. Is it my illness, this country or your dwindling spirit?

**COLIN** What?

**JAMES** That's magnetizing everyone.

**COLIN** I reckon the combo.

**JAMES** Hush!

**COLIN** What? (*They listen.*) Nothing.

**JAMES** Exactly. Good isn't it? No more Welsh chatter-boxing.

**COLIN** Fuck off!

**JAMES** How about me? Do I get a cuddle then?

**COLIN** A rare request. 'Course.

*They hug.*

**JAMES** The Derby and Joan of Essaouira. I like it here Colin. I really do. I like the climate. The people. The sea. Did you know I sneak off for midnight dips when you go wandering at all hours? (*COLIN shakes his head.*) I scoot down the beach past the hustlers and drunks and peel off and plunge in. No one can see me. And I can't see myself properly. My skin. My sores. This dreaded lurgi. I even fantasise about swimming across to the island.

**COLIN** To Mogador?

**JAMES** Yes. And it's all under the stars. My future and my past. I like the market, the food. The countryside. The sounds. Their sorcery. It all intrigues me. It's what keeps me going. That, and you.

**COLIN** You want to keep going?

**JAMES** I'm never sure. I worry about things. About you. Then tonight I heard your father arrive and I thought, "Good, I can let go now. He's got Shelley and Harry. They'll take care of him." Now it seems you have to nurse your father whilst Shelley drugs our maids.

**COLIN** Fucking slag-heap.

**JAMES** So. I can't let go after all.

**COLIN** He's like me. In the vortex. Tumbling off the edge of the world. He'll be alright. I hope.

**JAMES** Will you? Be alright?

**COLIN** Please don't ask me this now. Please. I feel like you're putting things in order.

**JAMES** I know everyone thinks I'm the selfish bastard, but a lot of the time I'm the one who takes care of you.

**COLIN** I know. I know. You're my mam and dad. My

brother. My friend, My lover. My keeper. You write the cheques. Show me how to be sophisticated. Of course, I won't be alright. But I'll be alright. I'll be alive.

**JAMES**  Tough.

**COLIN**  Don't! Please. Not tonight. Don't say anymore. I'm too tired. I'll just cry.

**JAMES**  From a half-cocked blow-job down the Gower.

*A silence.*

**COLIN**  I'm less naïve.

**JAMES**  And more moody.

**COLIN**  Sorry.

**JAMES**  You needn't be. It won't last.

**COLIN**  Hope not.

**JAMES**  Colin?

**COLIN**  James?

**JAMES**  Colin, I want to be cremated.

**COLIN**  Not tonight. Please. Please. Not tonight.

**JAMES**  Burnt like a log. Then get one of the fishermen to take me over to Mogador, full moon if possible, and let them scatter me over the island.

**COLIN**  How fucking epic.

**JAMES**  Freedom Colin. The fight to be free. A lot of those prisoners must have been petty thieves, small-time crooks, slaves, perverts. I bet they were treated foully. I bet there was a lot of whipping went on. There must be a lot of dancing spirits over there. Dancing for their liberation. I'd like to join in. And if the wind is good a little bit of me will float out to sea and who knows where I'll wash up?

**COLIN**   Down the bleeding Gower, I s'pose. You're a case you are James. You're like Christmas, New Year and the summer holidays all rolled into one.

**JAMES**   That's 'cos you've led me astray.

**COLIN**   I love you mate. I fucking love you. You can take Kezzy. Take him to the island with you. Freedom for all.

**JAMES**   Where is Kezzy?

*The cage is open and empty.*

**COLIN**   Where is he? Kezzy! Kezzy!

*SHELLEY enters.*

**SHELLEY**   Hiya. I've been waiting over by there. Sorry. I been listening. I wanted to come in earlier but... I was waiting for James to go to bed. Oh, I know James hears everything we says out here and I don't care. I got nothing to hide from James. You're a foul-mouthed old queer. But you haven't shut off. I like that. I let him go. I let him fly off.

**COLIN**   Why Shelley? Why?

**SHELLEY**   He had to. It was time.

**COLIN**   We were saving him.

**SHELLEY**   For what?

**JAMES**   Dinner.

**COLIN**   Shut up!

**SHELLEY**   I'm sorry. I had to let him go. It's what I had to do. I wanted to say sorry. 'Bout Aicha too. I'm a shabby little bitch. He can turn a few somersaults in bed, though boys. Well, Colin would know of course.

**JAMES** Me too.

**SHELLEY** What?

**JAMES** I'd know.

**SHELLEY** 'Bout what?

**JAMES** Ari. In bed.

**SHELLEY** Never!

**COLIN** James?

**JAMES** Not here. Way back. In London.

**COLIN** You bunch of whores.

**SHELLEY** Oh my God. Is he?

**JAMES** Relax. Negative. Funny that isn't it? Those who escape and those who don't.

**COLIN** Funny is hardly the word, eh, hardly the fucking word. Hang on. I've slept with Ari. I think my mam did. You have. Aicha. Now Shelley.

**SHELLEY** And sounds like your dad wants to.

**COLIN** How long have you been listening?

**SHELLEY** Forever. I heard the two of you. I know I'm a slag-heap. What can I say?

**COLIN** You can say we've all been had by Ari.

**SHELLEY** Cheeky Greek monkey.

**JAMES** You're a good fuck, Shelley. But a fucking awful nurse.

**SHELLEY** Fuck off. I read you bedtime stories. Give you hand-jobs. You've the life of Reilly.

**COLIN** You're a bunch of scumbags the lot of you. I should get on a camel and head to the desert.

**SHELLEY** Lawrence of Swansea.

**JAMES** I was thinking more Florence of Swansea.

**COLIN** Cheeky Welsh faggot. Common Swansea tart.

**SHELLEY** Screaming no-hoper.

**JAMES** Lover of Arabs.

*The clock strikes four. In the distance is the sound of cocks crowing. The noise gradually grows.*

**JAMES** Past my bedtime. I'll need a story Mum.

**SHELLEY** I'm not your mother.

**JAMES** Please Mum please.

**SHELLEY** Don't whine.

**COLIN** Can you hear those bloody cocks? I'll never fall asleep now.

**JAMES** When the cocks are up, Colin lies awake.

**COLIN** James. Tired.

**JAMES** You me or the joke?

**COLIN** The lot of us, eh Shell? The lot of us.

**SHELLEY** I dunno. What's it all about Alfie? What's it all about? Illness. Disease. Camaraderie. That's a good word innit? Sex. Promiscuity. Catholicism. Growing up. Growing old. Losing people. Making friends. Traipsing to the shops. Rainy weekends. Corns. Thrush. Face creams. Moslems. Jews. War 'n' peace. Having too much to drink. Not enough to eat. Feeling stupid when you've put your foot in it. Saying goodbye. Going on long trips. Going to strange places. Eating chips with strangers. Changing nappies. Having a good dump. Having an headache. Having a good swim on the beach. Barbecues. Going to the flicks. Sleeping like a baby.

*A pause. JAMES starts to cough. SHELLEY and COLIN look perturbed. They do nothing.*

**JAMES**   Letting birds have their wings. Not being afraid. Uprooting to bloody Morocco. Moving on. Trucking.

**COLIN**   It's about love. All about love. The search for love. The loss of love. Love unrequited. Love ignored. Love child. Love in bloom. Love fading. The thing we need. All we need. I am in love with Abderahim. Abderahim with the dirham. Aicha is in love with Ari. James the chameleon. Ari oddly enough loves me, but that isn't the same. And you Shell, who d'you love? Apart from Kezzy. Don't say. Don't spoil things now. Dad loves Mam and Mam ... well. Love passes. Love stops. Love returns. Love returned. When there is hope of love, there is hope. Love fulfilled. Love fulfilling. Loveful. Love full of love. Love love love love love.

*Quietly SHELLEY starts to sing.*

**SHELLEY** All you need is love,

>Dum da da da dum.

>All you need is love,

>Dum da da da dum.

*JAMES joins her.*

**JAMES**   Karma karma karma karma karma chameleon.

You come and go, you come and go oh oh oh.

*They are both singing in harmony and are joined by a chanting mullah. JAMES and SHELLEY turn to face each other, continuing their unison.*

**JAMES** Loving would be easy if your colours were like my dream, red gold and green, red gold and green.

**SHELLEY** Nothing you can do but you can learn how to be you

in time, it's easy.

Love is all you need,

Love is all you need,

Love is all.

*COLIN looks up at the night sky, almost squinting, searching, scouring the universe ... silence.*

*The End.*

**NEXT LESSON** by Chris Woodley
ISBN 978-1-912430-19-2   £9.99

**CARE TAKERS** by Billy Cowan
9781910798-81-2   £9.99

**THREE WOMEN** by Matilda Velevitch
ISBN 978-1-912430-35-2   £9.99

**PROJECT XXX** by Kim Wiltshire & Paul Hine
ISBN 978-1-906582-55-5   £8.99

**COMBUSTION** by Asif Khan
ISBN 978-1-911501-91-6   £9.99

**DIARY OF A HOUNSLOW GIRL** by Ambreen Razia
ISBN 978-0-9536757-9-1   £8.99

**SPLIT/MIXED** by Ery Nzaramba
ISBN 978-1-911501-97-8   £10.99

**THE TROUBLE WITH ASIAN MEN** by Sudha Bhuchar, Kristine Landon-Smith and Louise Wallinger
ISBN 978-1-906582-41-8   £8.99

**UNDER THEIR INFLUENCE** by Wayne Buchanan
ISBN 978-0-9536757-5-3   £6.99

**HARVEST** by Manjula Padmanabhan
ISBN 978-0-9536757-7-7   £6.99

**I HAVE BEFORE ME A REMARKABLE DOCUMENT** by Sonja Linden
ISBN 978-0-9546912-3-3   £7.99

**NEW SOUTH AFRICAN PLAYS** ed. Charles J. Fourie
ISBN 978-0-9542330-1-3   £11.99

**BLACK AND ASIAN PLAYS** Anthology introduced by Afia Nkrumah
ISBN 978-0-9536757-4-6   £12.99

**SIX PLAYS BY BLACK AND ASIAN WOMEN WRITERS** ed. Kadija George
ISBN 978-0-9515877-2-0   £12.99

More great plays at:
**www.aurorametro.com**